Engaging the Families of ELLs

Ideas, Resources, and Activities

Renee Rubin, Michelle H. Abrego, and John A. Sutterby

Routledge
Taylor & Francis Group
New York   London

First published 2012 by Eye On Education

Published 2013 by Routledge
711 Third Avenue, New York, NY 10017, USA
2 Park Square, Milton Park, Abingdon, Oxon OX14 4RN

Routledge is an imprint of the Taylor & Francis Group, an informa business

Library of Congress Cataloging-in-Publication Data

Rubin, Renee, 1954-
Engaging the families of ELLs : ideas, resources, and activities/Renee Rubin,
Michelle H. Abrego, John A. Sutterby.
        p.   cm.
Includes bibliographical references.
ISBN 978-1-59667-220-8
1. English language—Study and teaching—Foreign speakers.
2. English language—United States.
3. Language and languages—United States.
I. Abrego, Michelle H.
II. Sutterby, John A., 1966–
III. Title.
PE1128.A2R83 2012
428.0071—dc23   2012005661

Cover Designer: Dave Strauss, 3FoldDesign

ISBN: 978-1-596-67220-8 (pbk)

Also Available from EYE ON EDUCATION

Multicultural Partnerships:
Involve All Families
Darcy J. Hutchins, Marsha D. Greenfeld, Joyce L. Epstein,
Mavis G. Sanders, and Claudia L. Galindo

Reaching English Language Learners in Every Classroom:
Energizers for Teaching and Learning
Debbie Arechiga

School-Community Relations, Third Edition
Douglas J. Fiore

Write With Me:
Partnering With Parents in Writing Instruction
Lynda Wade Sentz

Family Reading Night
Darcy J. Hutchins, Marsha D. Greenfeld, and Joyce L. Epstein

Family Math Night:
Math Standards in Action
Jennifer Taylor-Cox

Family Math Night:
Middle School Math Standards in Action
Jennifer Taylor-Cox and Christine Oberdorf

Communicate and Motivate:
The School Leader's Guide to Effective Communication
Shelly Arneson

Wikis for School Leaders:
Using Technology to Improve Communication and Collaboration
Stephanie D. Sandifer

Dealing With Difficult Parents
And With Parents in Difficult Situations
Todd Whitaker and Douglas J. Fiore

About the Authors

Renee Rubin is an educational consultant living in the Rio Grande Valley of Texas. Her areas of specialization are literacy, English language learners, and family engagement. With the other authors, she designed and implemented an after-school program at a local elementary school in which undergraduate and graduate students interacted weekly with ELLs and their families. She also served as Co-Principal Investigator for a U.S. Department of Education Early Childhood Educator Professional Development Grant. She taught ELLs in elementary schools in New Mexico and Texas for 11 years and taught courses on how to enhance the literacy skills of ELLs to pre-service and in-service teachers at the University of Texas at Brownsville for 13 years.

Michelle H. Abrego is an associate professor at the University of Texas at Brownsville in the educational leadership program where she currently prepares principals and superintendents. Over the past 30 years she has served as a teacher, elementary and secondary principal, state program director for Safe and Drug Free Schools at the Texas Education Agency, and university faculty and program coordinator. Her public school experience includes serving in diverse urban school communities with large numbers of ELLs, primarily Latino students. Her passion for working with families of ELLs began with her doctoral dissertation and has continued throughout her university career where she works to prepare school leaders to engage ELL families. Most recently she has developed and implemented a course on family engagement of ELLs for school leaders and is working with aspiring and practicing school principals to increase the level of meaningful ELL family engagement at their respective campuses.

John A. Sutterby is an associate professor at the University of Texas at Brownsville in the area of early childhood education. His teaching experience at UTB has primarily been with Latino students. His research interests include outdoor play environments, bilingual education, and family involvement with Latino families. Dr. Sutterby has twice served as President of The Association for the Study of Play (TASP) as well as program chair for the Early Childhood Education/Child Development SIG for American Educational Research Association (AERA). He is currently serving as series editor for the Advances in Early Education and Day Care published by Emerald Publications. He is also a co-author of *The Developmental Benefits of Playgrounds*, published by Association for Childhood Education International (ACEI). His teaching experience has been primarily with Latino children in early childhood settings.

Table of Contents

Introduction

Engaging the Families of ELLs: Ideas, Resources, and Activities was written as a practical guide to facilitate the involvement of families of ELLs in the schools. Each chapter contains information and practical activities. The information, resources, and activities are provided so that readers can choose what best fits their situation. The scenarios in each chapter are based on actual experiences, successful and less successful efforts to engage the families of ELLs.

This book reflects the authors' philosophy that all families want the best education possible for their children and bring a variety of strengths to the educational process. Families participate in the education of their children in different ways, ranging from emphasizing the importance of education to their children to serving on district site-based decision making committees.

Schools should want all families, including families of ELLs, to participate in various ways. Families also have diverse expectations of schools. Rather than making assumptions about the schools or families, the authors have provided activities that will help schools decide how they would like to engage families and to find out the needs and wants of the specific families in their community.

Although the scenarios offer glimpses into cultural gaps that may occur with families of ELLs, efforts were made not to generalize based on language, ethnicity, or country of origin because there are too many variations within each group. The book does discuss ways to increase awareness, communication, respect, and trust in order to reduce cultural gaps.

Chapter 1 provides an overview of the benefits of engaging families in the schools, some of the challenges, and ways to meet those challenges. Chapter 2 discusses ways to find out what families really want for their children and from the school. Chapter 3 provides suggestions about how to make the school welcoming for all partners. Chapter 4 gives ideas for family meetings that go well beyond the traditional open house. Chapter 5 discusses improving communication with families through various means. Chapter 6 focuses on encouraging families to help their children at home. Chapter 7 tackles the topic of challenging situations involving families. Chapter 8 describes ways to find resources for effective family engagement.

This book emphasizes ideas and activities for families of ELLs because schools across the country have growing numbers of ELLs, and their families are often less engaged in the schools than families of native English speakers. We hope the book will be considered a resource for further involving families. Most of the ideas and activities presented will help better engage all families, not just those of ELLs.

1

Everyone Wins

Scenario
Arriving from Mexico

In the middle of November, Sandra Martinez arrived in Charlotte, North Carolina, from Monterrey, Mexico with her three children—Marco, age eight; Araceli, age six; and Margot, age three. They had just gotten their visas to join her husband who was working in the United States.

She was a little surprised and unprepared for the cold rain that greeted them on their arrival. Her husband met them at the airport and drove them to the small home he had rented for their arrival. Later that day, he drove them all to the local Walmart to purchase warm clothes.

After settling in, she knew her first task would be to take the older children to school. One of her neighbors, Victoria Mendoza, was a recent immigrant from Hidalgo, Mexico. Victoria offered to go with Sandra since she spoke enough English to translate for the newcomer family.

Marco and Araceli looked immaculate in their new school uniforms that their parents purchased at Walmart. As they walked up to Sallie Smith Elementary, they were a little nervous. The secretary seemed friendly as she handed over the many forms that had to be filled in and signed. The papers seemed endless. Finally, when they were all filled in, the secretary skimmed them and announced that Marco would be joining Ms. Parker's third-grade class while Araceli would be placed in first grade. The secretary then called an office, and they were joined by a tall, well-dressed woman. She was Ms. Anderson, the assistant principal.

"Ms. Anderson will be taking the children to their new classrooms," she said.

"Can't I go with them?" Sandra asked through the translator. "Sorry," Ms. Anderson replied. "Our school policy is to not let parents into the classrooms." Sandra looked worried. "They'll be fine," Ms. Anderson reassured her. "Vamos, let's go," she said to the children, who rose obediently and after hugging their mother, followed the tall woman out the door. Sandra was left with many doubts and concerns, which she shared with Victoria on the way home.

"I understand," Victoria replied. "But we have to adapt to the way they do things here."

New Immigrants in the United States Schools

It is easy to understand why schools don't want families walking into a classroom during instruction, but it is also easy to understand the parent's point of view. The parent is new to the country, doesn't speak English, and is used to a different education system. She wants to meet the children's teachers and see where they will be spending their days. What are some other ways this situation could have been handled? It can be difficult when schools have not had much experience working with immigrants who do not speak English.

New immigrants to the United States often have difficulty understanding the school system here. They often come with very different experiences in their home countries. It can be especially difficult if they do not speak English well. Much confusion can occur when school personnel are not prepared to work with families from differing linguistic and cultural backgrounds. Those of us who have grown up in the American school system may find the actions or decisions made by these families strange or unusual. They may be thinking the same things about us.

This can be seen in literature written by newcomers. Ernesto Galarza wrote in his autobiography, *Barrio Boy* (1988), how he had to adapt to American culture after he immigrated to the United States from Mexico:

> In more personal ways we had to get used to the Americans. They did not listen if you did not speak loudly, as they always did. In the Mexican style, people would know you were enjoying their jokes tremendously if you merely smiled and shook a little, as if you were trying to swallow your mirth. In the American style there was little difference between a laugh and a roar, and until you got used to them you could hardly tell whether the boisterous Americans were roaring mad or roaring happy. It was Dona Henriqueta more than Gustavo or

Jose who talked of these oddities and classified them as either agreeable or deplorable. (p. 205)

The significance of this for working with families of English language learners is that often we may find their cultural values and activities strange; at the same time, they will be evaluating our values and activities and finding them strange as well. Educators who understand this will better be able to help new immigrants make a smooth transition into school.

New immigrants like Sandra are proactive in dealing with the school system. One way they try to figure out the school system is to take advantage of local networks to help them navigate it. These may be other parents, community leaders, or religious leaders. New immigrants also seek out school personnel who speak their own language, whether they are custodians or school secretaries. The purpose of this text is to help educators better understand some ways they can help families make the transition to school. A smooth transition can help children better succeed.

Changing Demographics of America's Schools

Schools all across the nation are having to deal with influxes of immigrant students from all over the world. About one million new immigrants arrive in the United States each year. One quarter of these immigrants come from Mexico. Other large influxes in recent years have come from China, India, the Philippines, and Vietnam. Some states have had unique influxes of immigrants. In Minneapolis, Minnesota, for example, thousands of Somali refugees have settled, challenging the local schools to adapt to a different population. Detroit and parts of Michigan have seen growth in the number of Arabic speakers.

Immigrants have begun moving into states that have not always had large populations of non-English speakers. The five states with the fastest-growing percentage of immigrants are North Carolina, Nevada, Georgia, Arkansas, and Nebraska. Some states have attracted large numbers of immigrants seeking work in expanding industries. Arkansas and North Carolina have large chicken-processing facilities, and Nebraska has large meatpacking operations.

According to 2005–2006 data, there are 16 million children in the United States with at least one immigrant parent, twice the number in 1990. The states with the largest percentage of immigrant parents include California, Texas, New York, Florida, and New Jersey (Fortuny & Chaudry, 2009).

While Spanish is the most common language for English language learners, other common languages include Tagolog (spoken in the Philippines),

Vietnamese, several Chinese languages, and Japanese. Large cities like New York, Los Angeles, Chicago, and Houston have traditionally been magnets for immigrants. More than one hundred languages are spoken in the Houston Independent School District.

Benefits of Family Engagement

Family engagement brings many benefits to schools. Educational research over the past four decades has shown that higher rates of family involvement provide specific benefits for all members within the school community, including students, families, teachers, administrators, and community organizations and businesses. While some educators believe family engagement activities are too costly, research indicates that involved family members actually save schools money. An involved family member increases student academic achievement equivalent to the school spending an additional $1,000 on that one student (Houtenville & Conway, 2008). Students in particular reap many benefits when families are actively and consistently involved across all levels of schooling. Academic benefits from family involvement include higher grades, higher standardized test scores, higher graduation rates, and greater enrollment in postsecondary education. Higher rates of family involvement are also associated with increased readiness for school, enrollment in higher level programs, better school attendance, and higher rates of homework completion. Additional benefits of family involvement include improved behavior in school and at home, fewer special education referrals, and lower rates of juvenile arrest. Students whose families are involved also show more resilience and ability to persevere even in the face of obstacles.

Families themselves derive many benefits from engagement with schools. School involvement allows families to connect with other families in the school community and build supportive relationships. Such relationships provide a means for families to make new friends and become better informed about the school system and how it operates. It also provides an opportunity for families to learn about and access community resources. School involvement affords the opportunity for personal growth for family members. They may take the opportunity to improve their skills through adult education, English classes, and library use. Such engagement opportunities have been found to increase families' self-confidence in their ability to interact with schools and support their child's school efforts. This is an important benefit for families of English language learners, who may feel disconnected from the school and community due to differences in language and culture. It is critical that schools promote opportunities for families to connect to the school and the community. Without such efforts, many culturally and linguistically diverse families will be excluded from schools and miss the chance to build their own capacity to support their children's success.

Teachers often see the benefits of family engagement for the children or the families but don't realize that having families involved can make their job easier, too. Fourth-grade teacher Joan Young (2011) communicates some of these benefits to families. Families know the child best and can provide information that will be useful in teaching the child at school. For example, repeated ear infections as a toddler may result in difficulty hearing at school. When educators are aware of such issues, they can save time and provide children the needed assistance more quickly. A hospitalized grandmother may result in a child being withdrawn or tired during school. Without good communication with the family, teachers may assume that the child simply doesn't want to listen or participate in school. When teachers are aware of family situations, they can make appropriate accommodations. Students need to know that families and teachers are on the same team rather than being pitted against each other. If a strong relationship exists with the family, teachers and families can work together to resolve problems. For example, a child may need eyeglasses but a family doesn't want to admit to strangers that they can't afford them. If the teacher has open communication with the family, they can work together to find assistance to buy the glasses. Teachers and families working together have more power to get the services and materials that students need.

The school organization also derives many benefits from family involvement. Schools that have high levels of family involvement benefit from the increased level of trust between the school and families. Such schools report that parents have more confidence in the school and rank teachers higher. Additionally, these schools report higher levels of morale among teachers, better parental understanding of the role of the teacher, and a high level of respect for parents as the child's first teacher. Schools with involved families enjoy a better reputation in the community.

Schools benefit most when families are involved in activities that support student achievement. For example, family engagement efforts in the home centered on organizing and monitoring a child's time, supporting homework, and discussing school matters support academic success. Many schools do not value this informal support. School staff may place a higher value on formal support activities such as making copies, laminating materials, raising funds, and serving as chaperones for school trips. Research is clear that schools and families that work together see many benefits. Schools must reach out to linguistically and culturally diverse families in a variety of ways, which allow families and the school to be valued partners in student success.

All children benefit from family involvement regardless of their socioeconomic status, race, ethnicity, or their parents' education level. However, students who benefit the most from family involvement are those who are most at risk of not succeeding in school. Therefore, family involvement efforts must reach out to all families, including those who are culturally and linguistically diverse. Such families need support and encouragement and an active invitation from the school to become and stay involved. Without such efforts, schools lose the chance to reap the benefits of family involvement.

Engaging the Families of English Language Learners

The families of English language learners vary greatly, just as the families of native English speakers vary. Some families are limited to one or two parents and a child, while others have support from extended families, including grandparents, aunts, and uncles. Some parents have been divorced or divorced and remarried. Children may live with relatives other than their parents. Some families have high levels of education while others have had little opportunity to go to school. Beliefs about education and childrearing vary, too.

In addition to the differences that exist among all families, additional differences are present among English language learners. The number of years the families have been in the United States and their assimilation into American culture differ. Some families have friends or other family members who understand the U.S. education system, while others have to figure out the system on their own. Since most families of English language learners have only been in the United States for a few years, their expectations of schools, teachers, and parenting are more likely to reflect their home culture than those of the families of native English speakers.

The differences in expectations between families and schools may challenge effective family engagement. For example, many Mexicans have high regard for their teachers' knowledge and skills. Many think it would seem rude or presumptuous to ask questions about what happens in school or to try to teach their children at home. But American teachers who are not accustomed to this belief and expect families to be more involved in their children's education often see this respect as indifference.

Although some families of English language learners come to the United States for high-paying professional jobs, many are escaping poverty in their home countries and also face poverty here. Others had professional positions in their home countries but had to leave because of persecution, war, or other dangers. Arriving in the United States without strong English skills or U.S. certification in their fields, they had to accept manual labor jobs and work long hours to make ends meet. Some families barely have enough money for food and shelter. These families may not come to school because they cannot afford to lose wages, they lack reliable transportation or need to use costly public transportation, or they need to pay for someone to take care of babies or toddlers. Lack of money and time may mean families cannot check children's homework, take children to the library, or buy materials for projects. Families living in poverty also move more often in search of work and affordable housing, thus making it more difficult to develop ties with schools. Despite these limitations, most parents still care deeply about their children's education.

Due to the great diversity among all families and especially among those of English language learners, there is no one correct way to engage all families, but there are steps that can improve relations with these families. These are the steps:

♦ awareness
♦ communication
♦ respect

Awareness. Educators and administrators should become more aware of their own beliefs about the roles of families, teachers, and native languages in schools. Yet many times it is difficult to pinpoint one's own beliefs or how they might differ from other people's until confronted with those differing expectations and beliefs. Many areas differ among cultures and may impact family involvement: The role of the teacher in education and behavior management, the role of the family in the child's education and behavior at school, the importance of individual achievement versus teamwork, the emphasis placed on teaching English or the home language at school, the belief in fate or hard work as the cause of success, and the way time is treated (Lynch & Hanson, 2004).

In addition to being aware of one's own beliefs, it is important to understand some of the major cultural attitudes of the students' families. All families want the best for their children but what they consider to be the best and how to achieve it may differ from the views of the school. For example, one teacher approached a family with the great news that their child would probably qualify for the gifted and talented program. Instead of being excited as the teacher expected, the family was appalled because in their culture no one should strive to be better than anyone else. Greater awareness of the families' culture would have prevented this misunderstanding.

Schools may find it worthwhile to determine how benefits of family engagement are currently viewed by all stakeholders in the school community. This investigation is worthwhile as it may reveal that stakeholders are uninformed about the benefits of family involvement in the schools. And, more importantly, it may reveal that the family involvement efforts valued by the school are not valued by families or the community, especially culturally and linguistically diverse families. Results may further reveal that the family involvement efforts most valued by the school, such as fundraising, are not those that lead to increased student achievement. Becoming aware of current attitudes about families, especially culturally and linguistically diverse families, is an important first step in understanding how to increase the engagement of families of English language learners. The Views on Family Engagement activity at the end of the chapter can help raise awareness of everyone's views.

Teachers and staff who have been at the school for many years may also be able to provide some insight. Although families from the same linguistic and ethnic backgrounds differ in their beliefs, some families from similar backgrounds who already volunteer at the school or are fluent English speakers may shed light on the beliefs of more recent immigrants. An example of cultural and linguistic differences among families who may appear to be similar can be found in the authors' own work with a family literacy program along the Texas-Mexico border (Sutterby, Rubin, Abrego, 2007). Although almost all the families involved were Hispanic and lived in the same neighborhood, a close examination revealed many differences in family backgrounds within the program. Their situations included:

- ◆ recent immigrants from Mexico
- ◆ recent immigrants from Central America
- ◆ born and raised in the United States
- ◆ Spanish spoken at home
- ◆ English and Spanish spoken at home
- ◆ college-educated parents
- ◆ parents with little formal schooling
- ◆ varying levels of access to children's books

These differences might have been overlooked if the assumption was made that since the families were all Hispanic, they were alike.

Communication. Families can offer valuable information to teachers about students' health, previous education, interests, and other issues that may impact their experience in school. If two-way communication exists, educators and administrators can also become more aware of the expectations, strengths, and needs of the families. When the family does not speak English and the teacher does not speak the home language, two-way communication can be challenging. For simple messages about upcoming events or class activities, the child can be used as a translator, but for more complex messages about behavior or academic progress, someone outside the family is best.

Many families want to become more involved in their children's education, but they simply don't know how. Some also believe that they cannot help because they do not speak English well. In these cases, the schools must make an extra effort to reach out to the families and communicate that their knowledge and efforts to support their children's education are appreciated.

Respect. Sometimes schools don't value everything families do to support students. Even if the families don't come to school, they may emphasize the importance of a good education. They may check to make sure their children do their homework every night. One young teacher could not understand why more families didn't come to school. As she became older and had children of her own, she began to realize that parents were involved in their children's education simply by getting them to school on time every day. All families also have skills and knowledge that they share with their children even if it is not what is generally considered "school learning." For example, some families may not read books to their children, but they may tell stories, helping their children understand how stories are developed and increasing their children's vocabulary in their native language. Other families may teach their children skills, such as using herbs to treat illness, fixing cars, repairing plumbing, or decorating cakes. Some migrant children may have seen much of the country and can share their experiences with the class. Teachers and schools can build upon the children's home knowledge and experiences to help the student succeed in school. By valuing home knowledge, teachers can help establish relationships with families that are built on mutual respect.

Need for Teacher and Staff Professional Development

Research indicates that teachers and staff need more professional development in involving families, especially families of English language learners. Project Appleseed, an organization for parents interested in public school improvement, found that 77 percent of parents believed teachers should learn more about involving them in their children's learning. (See website on p. 12.) Research indicates that most teachers do not receive instruction in involving families either in their preservice education or their in-service professional development. Some of the possible areas for professional development are understanding families' communication styles, making families feel more comfortable at school, exploring what families can do at home to support their children's education, and learning how to involve families with minimal extra teacher time or effort.

Many of the activities and ideas in this book can be used with school personnel to build their capacity to successfully engage all families, including those who are culturally and linguistically diverse. The following activities and questions can be utilized as part of faculty and staff meetings throughout the year.

Activity
Views on Family Engagement

Purpose: This activity allows schools to investigate the attitudes of different stakeholders about family engagement and find out which types of family-school interactions each group values.

Participants: Families, teachers, administrators, school staff, community members, and middle school and high school students. Efforts should be made to collect information from as many people as possible, including secretaries, bus drivers, and custodians.

Preparation and Resources: Decisions should be made about what questions will be asked, what forms of communication will be used, who will participate in the study, how the findings will be analyzed, and how the results will be reported and to whom.

Description of Activity:
Questions. Schools can choose from the following questions or make up their own, but it is important that all stakeholders receive the same questions so that responses from different stakeholders can be compared.

- What should families do to support their children's education?
- What should teachers/schools do to communicate with families?
- What types of activities/meetings should teachers/schools have that involve families?
- What are the benefits of having families involved in schools?
- What should the teachers and the school do when a child repeatedly misbehaves at school or receives poor grades?
- What should the family do when their child repeatedly misbehaves at school or receives poor grades?
- What do you think is the strongest part of children's education at this school?
- If you could improve one thing at this school, what would it be?

Methods of Collecting Information. Written and online surveys allow respondents to remain anonymous and are usually easier to analyze than personal interviews, but many families may be reluctant or unable (because of lack of technology) to answer online surveys. In order to make sure families of English language learners are included in the responses, it may be necessary to meet with them in small groups and in their neighborhoods, such as at community centers or churches. Although this requires extra work, it may help educators receive responses from families who don't participate in traditional family activities, such as open houses or parent teacher organizations.

Analysis and Planning. If the effort is made to do an investigation, then the results should be analyzed and used for planning. How are school results similar or different from family or community responses? Results should also be compared to what is known about the benefits of different family engagement activities. For example, movie nights may develop a feeling of community and bring families to the school that would not otherwise be involved. But movie nights are unlikely to directly impact student achievement or school-family communication. Therefore, efforts should be made to include a wide range of family engagement activities in any plan.

Resources

Multicultural Books

Barrio Boy, by Ernesto Galarza (1972), was one of the first books written by a Mexican American immigrant about a child's perception of immigrating to the United States. His first-person account describes his life in Mexico around the time of the Mexican Revolution. His family decided to move to the United States to escape the war. His account chronicles the differences between life in Mexico and life in the United States, and although it takes place long ago, it still gives a child's-eye view of the immigrant experience that can be understood by a child today.

The Circuit, by Francisco Jimenez (1999), describes the life of a migrant farmworker in the 1950s and 1960s. Jimenez tells how his family enters the United States illegally in order to work. The family struggles to stay together under harsh conditions, and the children attend school as they learn to adapt to life in the United States.

My Diary from Here to There, by Amada Irma Perez (2009), is a picture book describing the trip a young girl and her family take from Ciudad Juárez in Mexico to California. The protagonist of the story keeps a diary about the experiences she has driving to Tijuana and then waiting there with family until the family's green cards are issued so they can cross to the United States.

Website

Need for more teacher professional development

www.projectappleseed.org/barriers.html

> This part of the Project Appleseed site is devoted to information about barriers to family involvement for both schools and families, including a lack of professional development for teachers in how to interact with families. Project Appleseed is an organization devoted to public school reform, especially through parental involvement.

Other Resources

Fortuny, K. & Chaudry, A. (2009). *Children of immigrants: Immigration trends, Fact sheet No. 1.* Washington, DC: Urban Institute.

Houtenville, A. J. & Conway, K. S. (2008). Parental effort, school resources, and student achievement. *Journal of Human Resources*, 43(2), 437–453.

Lynch, E. W. & Hanson, M. J. (2004). *Developing cross-cultural competence: A guide for working with children and their families* (3rd ed.). Baltimore: Paul H. Brookes.

Sutterby, J., Rubin, R., & Abrego, M. (2007). Amistades: The development of relationships between preservice teachers and Latino families. *The School Community Journal,* 17(1), 77–94.

Young, J. (2011/July). 8 reasons why parents should be involved at school/ TeacherTuesday. http://blog.volunteerspot.com/volunteer_guru/2011/07/ 8-reasons-parents-should-be-involved-at-school-teacher-tuesday.html

2

Finding Out What Families Want

Scenario
Investigating What Families Want

Hudde was president of the PTA at Roosevelt Elementary School in Austin, Texas. She was well-known for her boundless energy for participating at school. She visited the school nearly every day. She and her husband have lived in the same house two blocks from the school for nearly 20 years. The oldest of her six children was in high school while the youngest was just starting preschool. She worked in the mornings as a swim coach for a select swim team so that she could spend time at school during the day.

Hudde's work as president of the PTA made her indispensible to the school. The principal relied on her for fundraising activities and arranging parent volunteers. Fundraising was Hudde's strong suit. She had endless energy to ask for donations from local businesses. These were used as door prizes at the annual bingo night, which brought in the majority of funds for the PTA. She wasn't as successful with parent volunteers. When she first moved to the neighborhood, it was almost all single-family homes of professionals and workers in the local technology industry. Now, these families had moved away, and they had been replaced with renters from all corners of the world, many from Mexico, but also from El Salvador, Honduras, and Vietnam. So many Vietnamese had moved to the neighborhood that street signs were printed in both Vietnamese and English.

Ms. McGruder, the school principal, had been at the school for nearly 10 years, which was unusual for a district with a tradition of moving school administrators around. She had been there throughout much of the school's demographic shift from a majority white to a majority minority population. She hired as many bilingual teachers as she could get. She hired two Vietnamese aids and a Vietnamese-speaking secretary. Still, she worried about communication and parent participation in the school. Nearly all PTA members at the school were white women. PTA meetings were generally held in English, and less than 10 percent of families participated. The bingo night fundraiser, on the other hand, brought out nearly 1,000 participants at a school with only 600 children. Families from across the school took part; she noticed groups speaking Spanish, while some others spoke Vietnamese, and still others spoke English. She wondered how she could translate the enthusiasm of the fundraising night to other activities at school.

Meeting with Hudde after the fundraising night, Ms. McGruder brought up the topic. Hudde also was puzzled about how little participation there was in the PTA events compared to the excitement of the fundraising night. At the end of their meeting, Ms. McGruder and Hudde decided the best way to find out what all the parents wanted from the school was to investigate. With that, Hudde, with her famed energy for taking on difficult projects, was off to find out the best way to gather information about what families wanted.

Family Needs Assessment

Most schools think they do a good job reaching out to families. If asked how well they work with parents, schools will usually respond that they communicate fairly well and even offer several ways for parents to be involved in school life. Open houses, parent teacher conferences, written parent surveys, volunteer opportunities, and invitations to join parent teacher organizations are often identified.

These outreach activities may have little use for some families, especially those who are culturally and linguistically diverse. Does your school know what parents think about your school outreach efforts? How does your school find out what families want and need from the school?

The following is an actual conversation with a mother who had recently immigrated to the United States from Mexico with her four children. The parent was the mother of a child in the first-grade classroom of one of the author's graduate students. The mother was asked, "How have you been involved with the school as a whole, the principal, and the teacher?" The mother responded in Spanish with a description of her one and only attempt to attend a school parent teacher organization meeting:

We went one time to a meeting where there were several parents present, but we got up and left. The meeting was in English, and there was an argument. I think that they were attacking one another, and it just did not sound good. We do not like arguments. We had all the kids with us, and people (teachers and parents) were staring at us, so we left. We do not want to go to something like that again. [Translated from Spanish into English]

The same mother went on to describe another attempt at being involved with the school by going to a parent teacher conference:

We were invited one time to a parent conference to tell us that my son was not following the rules. We talked to my son, but we were still working on it. He had all S's on his report card, except for discipline. He is still having a hard time learning to follow the rules. We were never invited back because we [the family] all went, and my kids were upsetting the teacher. [Translated from Spanish into English]

Traditional school events such as a PTA meeting and a parent teacher conference proved to be an unfamiliar and negative experience for this mother. Chances are this parent will never attend another PTA meeting or come back for a parent teacher conference. How will the school ever know why she did not return or how she feels?

It is important that schools find a way to obtain input and feedback from all families, including those who may be unintentionally excluded by "traditional" outreach activities. A critical part of family outreach is finding out what *all* parents want and providing parents with opportunities to let the school know what they can do better.

Surveys

Many different types of surveys are administered to families. Some of these surveys aim at finding levels of satisfaction with current practices. For example, surveys often ask families to rank how well the school keeps all families informed about important issues and events or how well a child's teacher keeps parents informed about how the child is doing in school. These surveys often list a current practice such as parent teacher conferences and ask parents to rate their feelings about this practice as very dissatisfied through very satisfied. Results from this type of survey can be easily tabulated and included in required reports.

Washoe School District in Reno, Nevada, conducts a needs assessment of parents in English and Spanish at each of its schools. Parents are asked to complete a 25-question survey. About half the items on the survey are ranked on a five-point Likert scale from strongly disagree to strongly agree. A few examples are, "My child's school sees parents as important partners" and "My child's school wants to hear my ideas about how to make the school better." Remaining items ask for a yes or no response or ask parents to check which answer applies. For example, parents are asked, "Do you have Internet access at home?" Or they are asked, "Where do you get most of your information about school?" This specific question is followed by a list of items, such as e-mail, child's folder, newsletter, etc. Parents are asked to check the one item. (See websites.) Once the surveys are distributed and collected, the district compiles results for each school. One hint for schools administering surveys is to enlist the help of a local university to asssemble and analyze the results. The Washoe School District contracted with the Center for Program Evaluation at the University of Nevada–Reno for this purpose.

The Kentucky Department of Education's website has a portion of the site devoted to sample needs assessments that have been administered by various preschools around the state. (See websites.)

The above examples provide schools with a good starting point for a general assessment of schools' strengths and weaknesses and allow for the comparison of results from year to year or across schools in a district. This type of survey does not help identify the specific practices that create satisfaction or dissatisfaction with the school. For example, a parent might say they are satisfied with parent teacher conferences but it could be for many reasons, including length of the conference, scheduling options, the teacher's attitude, or a glowing report on their child. Surveys about current practices also fail to gain input about needs that are not currently being met.

In order to get more detailed input from families, it is important that surveys are in the family's home language and that at least some of the questions are open-ended to allow families to provide more detailed answers than "very satisfied." For example, families may be asked, "What would you like to learn more about related to your child's education?" It is too easy for schools to plan out family involvement activities for the year based on what they think parents need. Far too often assumptions are made about the needs of the culturally and linguistically diverse families that may not at all be what families want. There is a difference between soliciting input on how well a school shares information it has decided parents should know and gathering information from all families about what they would like to learn about the school or how the school could support their parenting efforts.

Parenting materials frequently suggest the need to gather parental input on specific school policies or curriculum revisions, such as school uniforms or year-round schooling. Although family input is important on these issues, it is vital to make sure that families are well informed on the various advantages and disadvantages before soliciting family input. This might be done through forums held in community centers, churches, or other gathering points as well as in the school. For example, some school districts began year-round schools with the backing of the parents only to find them opposing the innovation a few years later. Before the year-round schools began, the families did not understand that year-round schools usually have weeks off in fall or spring when other schools are in session. This makes finding child care for young school-aged children difficult.

There also may be some topics that are not appropriate for family surveys or are appropriate for only some families. For example, some online surveys ask families about No Child Left Behind, which even Congress has struggled to fully understand. Most parents also do not have the experience or knowledge to compare one reading or math program with another. One school survey asked all parents about the exit exam given to high school seniors. If families did not include someone who had already taken the exit exam, their opinions were unlikely to be well-informed. Specific surveys can be created for different families. For example, the families of seniors could receive a survey about how well prepared their child was for the exit exam, graduation, and the future. This survey could also solicit ideas for ways of better preparing future students. Families who just registered a child in the school district could receive surveys about the registration process.

Well-intentioned surveys to gather parent feedback may actually serve to marginalize parents in culturally and linguistically diverse families. Here are some examples that illustrate this point.

Recently, a suburban school district in the southwestern United States ran a newspaper column in which it invited its parents to provide input on four questions related to professional learning communities (PLCs) in their children's school. Parents were asked: 1.) What do we want children to learn? 2.) How will we know if they have learned? 3.) What will we do if they don't learn? and 4.) What will we do if they already know it?

The same article encouraged parents to go online to the district's homepage and make use of a tab that linked parents to the district's curriculum management guide. The guide outlined what students would be learning across grade levels in various subjects and illustrated how the curriculum spiraled. Parents were to review the curriculum units and ask questions about homework and classwork in order to answer two of the four PLC questions. The district website was all English with one video in Spanish.

Demographics in this district indicated that 17.9 percent of students were English language learners (ELLs). The district's approach to reach out to parents would most likely work for families who spoke English; had a strong working knowledge of the American school system; had access to newspapers, computers, and the Internet; and had time to search the district's website. Families without such a background would be excluded from involvement in the district's PLC. It is highly unlikely that linguistically diverse families would participate in the districtwide PLC discussion. (See websites.)

A PTA at an elementary school recently gave an online survey to its parents related to PTA efforts to support the school. Each item on the survey was to be ranked as a priority, acceptable, or not a concern. Areas surveyed included school book fairs, classroom volunteers, Dr. Seuss's birthday celebration, field day, teachers' Christmas wish lists, and e-mail as a means of communicating with the PTA. The survey was well intentioned, but would be meaningless for families unfamiliar with American schooling and culture and those who did not speak English.

In both examples, culturally and linguistically diverse parents could possibly be labeled as unsupportive of efforts to improve the school because they did not participate in surveys. The reality is that these parents want their children to succeed in school but may not know how to participate in the manner the school wants or expects.

Schools administering surveys must look carefully at the questions posed and ensure that they are meaningful for all parents and families. A team of parents, teachers, community members, and administrators may wish to carefully review any parent needs assessments before they are sent out to ensure that they are inclusive of all families in the school community.

Beyond Surveys

Methods other than traditional surveys about existing school practices should be used by schools so that input is collected from all families. Teachers may ask parents in person what topics they would like to learn about. This information can be asked of parents when students are dropped off in the morning, picked up from school, or at any time the opportunity presents itself. People are often more honest when they are not putting things down in writing. Such feedback allows the school to identify the information and services that all families want and need.

For example, one time we (the authors) were working with a local elementary school on an afterschool reading program. Various literacy topics were considered for families. It would be easy to assume that since the families did not speak English, were recent immigrants, and came from high-poverty households that literacy practices did not take place in the home and perhaps parents themselves needed to learn to read and write or be shown how to read to their children and make books available for them. However, in talking with the parents over several weeks time, parents expressed a strong interest in the states' early literacy assessment that was being used in the school and wanted to learn about what it was and how it would be used to monitor their children's progress. It is unlikely that this information would have been gathered from a written or online survey sent out to parents.

School office staff can be trained to solicit information from parents about their needs when students are registered for school, picked up for doctor's appointments, and so on. Parent liaisons can also serve as valuable resources in helping obtain information from parents, including suggestions for how the school can better meet their needs. Such conversations with school staff send the message that the school is open and receptive to parental input from all families.

Parents themselves can help obtain information from other families. Find families who are willing to contact other families with children in the same school and collect information from them. In this way, information may be obtained from families who do not come to the school or complete written surveys. Some schools use parent volunteers who are willing to give out their phone number so that parents may call them with questions about school. Parent volunteers can keep track of questions and concerns and share them with the school.

Administrators can solicit information from parents when various types of parenting meetings are held such as PTA meetings, parent coffees, home visits, etc. Principals may even consider hosting a specific activity such as lunch with the principal with the specific purpose of hearing from families about the topics they are interested in learning.

Some schools also solicit information from middle school and high school students. In this way, the school can find out about what the students may be telling their families about teaching, discipline, homework, and student relations.

Focus groups are another way of soliciting information from families. This is a method of gathering information used by private marketing firms that can also be applied in schools. An informal group of 6 to 12 family members may be chosen for their specific knowledge or background. For example, a focus group could be formed with families of ELLs of Somali background and a translator could be present to moderate the discussion. General questions could be asked about what successes their children were having and what they thought might be improved. Participants respond not only to the moderator but also to each other. These informal discussions often elicit information that might not come to light on surveys or in one-on-one interviews. Of course, these focus groups only represent the opinions or beliefs of a small group of people, and some people may be afraid to discuss their true feelings because the discussions are being recorded or because of other members of the focus group.

At the classroom level, teachers can gain valuable insight into their children's daily lives and families. One activity utilized by a second-grade teacher is the "All About Me" book. Students complete the book at the beginning of the school year. Simple questions or sentence frames are provided for students to respond to in their book. The students also include drawings and writings of their own. Teachers may ask a variety of questions: "How many brothers and sisters do you have?" "Draw a picture and label your family members that live with you." "Do you have any pets?" "What is your favorite part of school?" "What things are hard for you at school?" "What do you like to do in your free time at home?"

The "All About Me" book can be modified to meet the child's level of development and used at many grade levels. The more that schools can learn about their students and families, the better they will able to partner with them in promoting student success.

Topics of Interest

It is important to ask general questions to find out about the needs and wishes of families and children without limiting them to issues that the school considers important. For example, families may be asked what the school could do better. The answers to this general question may include ideas that had not been previously considered by the school. For example, some families may want the school to be open 30 minutes earlier so they can bring their child to school before leaving for work, others may want a health clinic to be associated with the school, and still others may want their children to have music time and would be willing to volunteer their services to teach songs. Each of these suggestions provides both challenges and opportunities that may not have previously been considered by the school.

In addition, the school may want to ask questions about specific topics of interest. These will vary from school to school but some suggestions include homework, discipline, bullying, grading, extracurricular activities, transportation, safety, and communication.

Schools wishing to gather input from all families may use written needs assessments and surveys as a starting point. However, these assessments and surveys need to be administered in a variety of formats to ensure that culturally and linguistically diverse parents have a voice in the school. The activities listed later in this chapter will help schools improve their efforts to carry out a thorough needs assessment that reaches all families.

Educators should be careful to not label certain families as uninterested in their children's education because they do not attend traditional school events such as PTA meetings and parent teacher conferences or fill out school surveys. Families may appear disinterested because they have difficulty being involved in activities which they don't understand and have little or no meaning to them. Schools must make it a priority to learn from all families. The perspectives of "hard to reach" families on parent involvement efforts will yield valuable information on how to improve such efforts and build meaningful partnerships.

Comprehensive Planning

Schools should develop a comprehensive plan or approach for conducting the family needs assessment in their school community. The initial step involves determining how well the school currently conducts needs assessments of families. The activities at the end of the chapter will be helpful in making this determination. Additionally, the activities will help schools modify existing surveys and select appropriate formats for soliciting input from all families. A neighorhood assessment sample is provided.

When possible, seek the assistance of community agencies, civic groups, and faith-based organizations in the school attendance area to plan, advertise, and implement the school's comprehensive needs assessment. These organizations may be able to conduct family focus groups for the school. They may also encourage and increase family participation in written surveys. Volunteers may offer to administer the surveys orally and record the results for families uncomfortable with writing. Diverse families may also feel more comfortable participating in the needs assessment outside the school setting in locations such as community centers, churches, temples, or mosques.

A timeframe for the needs assessment should be established and plans developed for how the data will be compiled and analyzed. Decide in advance if the district is able to provide support to the school on this step or if the services of an outside organization will be needed. The results of the needs assessment should be shared with the community in the appropriate languages and utilized to develop a plan of action to build a stronger relationship with all families, especially those that are culturally and linguistically diverse.

Activity
Analyze School Needs Assessment Practices

Purpose: The purpose of this activity is to determine how well the school gathers and solicits information from all families in the school community, including those who are culturally and linguistically diverse.

Participants: School faculty and staff

Preparation and Resources: Run off the list of questions below. Have copies of any current needs assessment the school uses available as a reference.

Description of Activity: Assemble school staff and ask them the questions below in an effort to determine the current status of the campus in assessing the needs of all families. Divide the faculty and staff into small groups to review the questions. Each group should have a member assigned to record the responses. After each group has answered the questions, the responses should be shared with the entire group. At the closing of the discussion, arrangements should be made to analyze the responses, discuss them with staff members, and write a plan based on the information.

Does your campus conduct a needs assessment of families?

- If so, how is it done?
- Why is the needs assessment conducted?
- How and with whom are the results shared?
- What changes have occurred at your school as a result of the needs assessment?
- If the school conducts needs assessments, do families just comment on current practices or is there an opportunity to suggest new ideas or express concerns on different topics?
- What overall percentage of school families provide input regarding their wants and needs?
- To what extent are families of English language learners a part of the overall percentage of family input?
- Describe the typical family in your school? Does one exist?
- Does your school hold expectations for family engagement that center around traditional mainstream families? Explain your response. (Recall that this question was posed in Chapter 1 when examining how each group of stakeholders may hold differing views regarding which benefits of family involvement are the most valued.)
- What changes need to be made to ensure that the needs and wants of all school families are integrated into the school and surrounding community?
- Whose responsibility is it to make changes that increase the involvement of all families, including those who are culturally and linguistically diverse?

Options: Conduct the same activity with a cross section of stakeholders, including parents, community members, and staff. Compare the results of each group's discussion, and use the results to help develop a comprehensive needs assessment for the campus.

Activity
Focus Groups

Purpose: Focus group interviews allow schools to obtain more in-depth information from selected families. Although more information is revealed in these group interviews than in most written surveys, as a practical matter fewer families can be contacted.

Participants: Family members from a particular cultural and linguistic group should be selected.

Preparation and Resources: Prepare focus group questions in advance; identify school faculty or community members to conduct the interview and to record family responses. (A university may be helpful in providing someone who speaks the native language of the families being interviewed. Volunteers are needed to conduct the interview and record responses.)

Description of Activity: A variety of questions may be asked of parents during the interviews. Here are some possibilities:

- In what parent involvement opportunities have you participated at your child's school? Describe your experience.
- What barriers exist that hold you back from participating more in your child's school?
- What suggestions do you have for how the school could increase parental involvement?
- Is there anything else that you would like to tell us?

After the interviews are conducted, summarize the responses, and share them school faculty and staff. Use the information to determine what changes are needed in parental engagement efforts to reach out to all families. Repeat the focus group as needed to accomodate as many cultural and linguistic groups as are part of the school community.

Note of caution: Questions for the focus groups should be modified as needed to ensure they are culturally sensitive. Feedback should be solicited from a parent or community member who represents the cultural and linguistic group being interviewed to assure questions are culturally sensitive.

Resources

Multicultural Books

Josias, Hold the Book, by Jennifer Riesmeyer Elvgren (2006), is a picture book that describes a boy growing up on a farm in Haiti. He has to work on the farm to help support his family, so he cannot go to school. Josias is responsible for growing beans in the garden but has difficulty doing it. In the end, he asks how school might help him learn to farm better. His family agrees to let him study in school so he can come back and help the family with the farm.

Tomas and the Library Lady, by Pat Mora (2000), is a picture book based on the experiences of Tomas Rivera, whose family were migrant farmworkers. Tomas grew up to become an influential educator and author. This book shows how an attentive librarian is able to reach out to a child who did not have had access to books.

Websites

Parent Needs Assessment

www2.ed.gov/admins/comm/parents/parentinvolve/report_pg18.html

> The U.S. Department of Education's webpage for *Engaging Parents in Education: Lessons Learned from Five Parental Information and Resource Centers*. This link is specific to assessing local needs of parents and provides valuable information on conducting a needs assessment along with examples of surveys and results from various school districts.

Parent Involvement Needs Assessment Sample

www.washoe.k12.nv.us/parents/parent-involvement/
> parent-involvement-needs-assessment
> This is the Parent Involvement Needs Assessment page for the Washoe School Distict in Reno, Nevada.

Parent Self Assessment

www.projectappleseed.org/reportcard.html

> The Parental Involvement Report Card page of the Project Appleseed website offers parents the opportunity to rank their own involvement efforts in their child's school through a 30-question survey and a video pop quiz. The home page for Project Appleseed is www.projectappleseed.org. This quiz is unique as it allows parents to grade themselves on their efforts to be involved in their children's school.

Preschool Parent Surveys

www.education.ky.gov/kde/instructional+resources/preschool/for+preschool+
coordinators+and+teachers/parent+survey.htm
The Kentucky Department of Education's Instructional Resources page for preschool parent surveys

Professional Learning Communities

www.littleelmjournal.net/articles/2011/10/26/little_elm_journal/news/9017.txt
News article from the *Little Elm Journal* about district efforts to engage parents in
professional learning communities

Other Resources

Delgado Gaitan, C. (2004). *Involving Latino families in schools: Raising student achievement through home-school partnerships.* Thousand Oaks, CA: Corwin Press.
The Promise Neighborhood Institute provides a needs assessment at
http://www.promiseneighborhoodsinstitute.org/policylink_pni/How-to
-Build-One/Planning-a-Promise-Neighborhood/Data/Needs-Assessment/
(language)/eng-US

3

Creating a Welcoming
School Environment

Scenario
Families Not Welcome

Mrs. Fu hurried up the front steps to her daughter's school, Jefferson Elementary, her five-year-old, Hui Li, in tow. Hui Li and her mother were attending the school's kindergarten round-up taking place that day. Jefferson Elementary had designed a spring informational meeting for all kindergartners who would be enrolling in the school that fall. Mrs. Fu had taken time off from the family business to attend the meeting. A neighbor in her apartment building who had a child the same age as Hui Li had told her she needed to go if she wanted to make sure that Hui Li had a good teacher for kindergarten.

Mrs. Fu had never been to the school. She had driven by it many times but knew little about it. The school marquis posted various announcements about school events but she read little English and was unsure of the terminology she saw, such as "New York State Assessment Testing today" or "PTA meeting tonight."

Mrs. Fu nervously entered Jefferson Elementary's main corridor and stood silently with her daughter at her side. She looked around for some sign of where to go for the meeting. Numerous people wearing name badges walked by. She was sure that she must look out of place, but no one said anything to her or greeted her. After a few minutes, she made the decision to walk down the hallway in search of information about the meeting's location as she didn't want to be late.

Finally, a man approached her and told her that she could not be in the hallway without a name badge and that she must sign in at the school's office and pointed in the opposite direction and walked away. Mrs. Fu turned toward the direction in which the man had pointed and made her way to the school's office. The man had not even asked her if she needed help. The school office was a busy place. Everyone there seemed hard at work, and no one even looked up as she entered. She didn't want to disturb them so she sat down quietly on a bench to wait. Mrs. Fu glanced nervously at her watch as she was sure she'd be late for the meeting.

After 10 minutes, Mrs. Fu approached the office counter and waited quietly. Finally, a clerk looked up and asked her what she needed. Mrs. Fu tried to explain in English to the best of her ability that she was there for a meeting about her daughter and kindergarten. The clerk mentioned that she wasn't sure about any meetings that day, but she'd find out if she could wait just a minute. Mrs. Fu sat back down and waited another five minutes until the clerk had time to call a kindergarten teacher's class-room and inquire about the meeting. As she was waiting, a well-dressed man with a briefcase walked by and greeted the office staff and walked into the principal's office. By this time, Mrs. Fu felt extremely self-conscious. She felt like she had interrupted the busy pace of the office and was bothering the school. She had hoped she'd get to meet the principal and introduce Hui Li. This would be her chance to request a good teacher for her daughter.

Her thoughts were interrupted as the clerk called out to her to tell her the kinder-garten meeting had taken place the day before. Mrs. Fu didn't know what to do. Hui Li's smile disappeared as her mother explained in Mandarin Chinese that there was no meeting at school that day for kindergarten. Quietly, Mrs. Fu and her daughter got up and left Jefferson Elementary School. She mentally made plans to ask her neighbor what she should do about how to get into kindergarten.

Scenario
All Families Welcome!

Irma Rosales was very excited about the upcoming school year. Just yesterday two faculty members from the neighborhood school, Madison Elementary, stopped by to greet the family and extend their wishes for a wonderful school year. Her local parish priest had announced at the church that staff from Madison Elementary School would be doing a neighborhood walk to meet families and share school information.

The teachers hadn't stayed long—only about 10 minutes. They brought a "wel-come gift" for the family—a folder embossed with the name of the school and impor-tant contact information, including phone numbers and e-mail addresses. In addition to the folder, the family received Madison Elementary's calendar for the year and a refrigerator magnet shaped like a school with important school phone numbers for easy access. All the information was published in both Spanish and English.

At the visit, the teachers explained in Spanish that they were doing a neighbor-hood walk and wanted to make sure that everyone knew when the first day of school was, how to register for school, and how to get in touch with the school if they had any questions. The teachers seemed genuinely interested in meeting her twins, Mary and Juan, who would be attending school for the first time. Mrs. Rosales was relieved to be able to ask some questions about the prekindergarten program. The teachers explained that Madison was able to help families make connections to community agencies and services. The Madison teachers also took the time to ask what needs the school could assist her with and what topics she'd be interested in learning about related to the school.

Mrs. Rosales later thought about the information she had learned during the visit: how to register her children for school and the date Madison would host a "Meet the Teacher Saturday" prior to the school year starting. She was relieved that she would have the opportunity to see her children's classroom and meet her children's teachers before the school year started. Perhaps most of all, she was excited that the school had a school-based mobile health unit available to provide physicals and immunizations. The clinic would allow her to get the twins' immunizations up to date before the start of school.

Her neighbors were right. The local elementary school loved and cared about its students. She could rest easier knowing that she could trust the school with her twins and was glad people at the school spoke Spanish.

Importance of School Climate

Jefferson Elementary School and Madison Elementary School each made the effort to reach out to families before the school year started. However, the outcomes were very different.

Mrs. Fu's experience with Jefferson Elementary left her discouraged and confused. Her intentions to register her daughter for kindergarten, get a good teacher, and meet the principal were met with disappointment. Nothing worthwhile or productive emerged from her contact with the school. Her time and efforts were wasted. The school sent the message that it was much too busy to deal with Mrs. Fu and that she would need to figure out how the school operated and comply with its operating procedures. The school climate was cold and unwelcoming to families who were unfamiliar with its routines and procedures and did not speak English well.

In stark contrast, Mrs. Rosales's first encounter with Madison Elementary was very positive and productive. Madison Elementary was able to furnish

Mrs. Rosales with critical school information on starting dates, events, and health services. The school asked questions and demonstrated a genuine interest in her children. It was clear that the school wanted families involved as they came to her home and visited with the parish priest.

Madison Elementary sent out a clear message to Mrs. Rosales that families were important and valued by the school. Now, even before families came to the school building for the first time, they could be confident the school would be happy to see them and welcome them. Its outreach was deliberately and intentionally planned to engage families who did not speak English and or lacked familiarity with American schooling. Scheduling a Saturday back to school event versus a weekday or weeknight event was aimed at meeting the needs of working families. Madison Elementary School was ready and willing to build a relationship with its school community, including diverse families.

Making schools a welcoming place is critical to families who are culturally and linguistically diverse. Schools can be viewed as intimidating places at odds with families' native culture, language, and values or they can be viewed as welcoming places that help families and acknowledge diversity. Such schools do not ignore differences in language and culture. Instead, they acknowledge, learn about, honor, and value these differences. Schools wishing to engage families of English language learners must send a clear and sincere message that they are interested in partnering with them in a meaningful way to make schooling a successful experience. Schools convey such a message by providing a welcoming climate filled with positive interactions between the school and the family.

What Makes a Welcoming School?

It is important to remember that families have contact with a variety of school staff, not just family liaisons, teachers, and principals. Any efforts that are made to learn more about a school's climate should include secretaries, receptionists, guidance counselors, cafeteria workers, security guards, school nurses, librarians, custodians, crossing guards, bus drivers, and so on.

As parents and educators, we have visited and worked in dozens of schools at all levels. We have found that there are vast differences among schools in how they approach families and visitors. We have all been through many varieties of identity checks and sign-in procedures. Many schools today have electronic gates. We have had many different experiences when requesting information from school staff. Some of us have even gotten lost looking for the office at a particularly complex campus. We have also had the experience of being ignored while standing in the school office waiting for staff to assist us.

The registration process is particularly important because it is often the first contact a family has with the school. One of the authors recently helped a friend who had just moved to the neighborhood register her son for high school. We went to the high school and were told to go to an intake center. We went to the intake center armed with a birth certificate and vaccination records. The intake center said they required a water or electric bill to prove the child lived in the area served by the school. These were the only documents that would suffice. We returned to her house and finally located a water bill and returned to the intake center. With the paperwork from the intake center, we returned to the school where we were sent to the nurses' office, which took about 10 minutes to find. The nurse cleared the student, and we waited to see a counselor to set up his schedule. He didn't have transcripts from his last school, so she made a tentative schedule until the transcripts arrived. She told the student he could come to school the next day. One can only imagine what this experience would be like for a family who did not speak English, did not have a car, or did not have up-to-date vaccination records.

Take a minute to think about how an outsider might approach your school. What sort of knowledge would you need in order to access your school? What sort of information can you get from signs around campus, especially if you do not speak English? What sorts of barriers are there for people who want to participate in school functions? How are staff trained to greet visitors to the school? What sorts of routines like registration or vaccinations would families need to know? As insiders we often assume the answers to these questions are simple, but often to outsiders the answers are not so obvious.

Schools need to examine all interactions that occur between school employees and families. School staff should "walk" through a school day as a family member in order to identify all the school employees with whom they come into contact. For example, when family members bring students to school in the morning, with whom do they interact? If families visit the school during the day, with whom do they come in contact? Do they interact with office staff, security guards, or cafeteria workers? Are these interactions positive and welcoming?

Schools may wish to use a "mystery shopper" to evaluate the school's interactions with families. This means a visitor comes to the school to see how he or she is treated and determine to what extent the school climate is welcoming. Using a mystery shopper helps schools examine how visitors who do not speak English or are unfamiliar with American schooling are treated. Schools should not assume that faculty and staff possess the needed skills to make schools family friendly. Businesses often undertake extensive training in customer relationships. Schools should do the same.

New York City schools researched how to become friendlier for immigrant families in an effort to increase their involvement in the schools. Immigrant parents' interviews revealed that unwelcoming school staff made entry to the school difficult and uncomfortable for them. In particular, the school security guards did not interact well with immigrant parents who did not have a driver's license for identification. As a result, parents chose to stay away from the school. A recommendation that emerged from the study was to offer parent friendliness training modules as professional development for all faculty and staff. (See websites.)

New educators should be provided background on the school community and its families as part of its new teacher induction programs. Taking a bus tour of a school or a district's attendance zone is recommended as part of an exemplary new teacher induction program (Wong, 2003).

Ramirez and Soto-Hinman (2009) expand on the idea of bus tours for new teachers and encourage teachers to travel into the community to learn about the culture of the community and its members. Traveling throughout the community provides educators with insight about children's home life, background, and culture. Educators might want to take community field trips several times throughout the year. After the trips, school faculty should discuss what they've observed and learned about the community. Such trips increase familiarity with the community and increase the level of respect the faculty has for school families and the rich array of experiences brought to school each day. Faculties may also extend the discussion to include the types of community festivals and cultural events that occur and identify assets (rather than deficits) within the community. Such trips and discussions allow faculty and staff to become more familiar and comfortable with families different from themselves. As a result, schools are made more welcoming for all families.

Schools may wish to evaluate their climate by using a specific checklist that covers items related to making families feel welcome at the school. One such checklist, called "Schools That Say Welcome," is from a guide published by the Wisconsin Department of Instruction entitled *Organizing a Successful Family Center in Your School: A Resource Guide.* Appendix B (pp. 27–28) contains the "Schools That Say Welcome" checklist. Schools may use the checklist to rate how welcoming the school is to families. Items from the list include

office staff are friendly and courteous to parents and other visitors on the phone and in person; a welcome sign and school map are displayed near the school entrance; and the school has a family center or another place where information about children's learning, school programs, and community resources are easily available

The guide may be downloaded from http://dpi.state.wi.us/fscp/pdf/fcsprntc.pdf.

Welcoming checklists such as this one can be modified to focus on school climate for families who speak little or no English. For example, the measure on friendly and courteous office staff can be extended to include whether the office staff has been sensitized to linguistic needs of parents or whether office staff speak the parents' native language. Survey items about school signs and maps can ask if these items are posted in languages other than English. Schools can also determine not only that information on school programs and community resources is available but also if it is available in languages other than English.

Schools may also want to use the *Family Friendly Schools Guide*, published in English and Spanish by the Washoe County School District in Reno, Nevada. (See websites.) The guide is intended to be used by a family friendly school team made up of a school administrator, faculty, and support staff with parents, students, and community representatives. Together, the team can examine the school's physical environment, including the office area, front entrance/lobby, and exterior of the building to ensure that it is warm and inviting. The guide also has a section on school climate in which the school atmosphere is measured in terms of how welcoming the school is to visitors, the level of customer service provided, and the perceptions of the school community, for example "our school has a trusting climate where parents feel comfortable bringing concerns and suggestions to school including a suggestion box, brief surveys, informal opportunities for parents to speak with staff/members and/or other means" (p.4). The family friendly team scores the various sections of the guide to identify areas of strength and areas in need of improvement. The results can then be used to build an action plan to make the school more welcoming to all families including those who are culturally and linguistically diverse. (See www.washoe.k12.nv.us/docs/pdf/FamilyFriendlyGuide-WebsiteSept061.pdf.)

Safe Schools

A safe and orderly school environment is an indicator of a positive and welcoming school climate. Attendance rates are higher at schools that are perceived as safe. Schools should know if family members feel that all students feel safe, secure, and comfortable at the campus.

All other efforts to involve families in schools will fail if students and families do not feel the school is safe. A study of 900 parents from a wide variety of socioeconomic statuses and ethnic communities across San Francisco indicated that their number-one priority in selecting a school was a safe place to learn. (See other resources on p. 50.) Schools need to prioritize safety, have processes in place to prevent and deal with unsafe situations, and have fair discipline policies that are consistently enforced throughout the school program, including in the cafeteria, on the bus, in the gym, and during after-school activities. All students should be involved in programs to promote self-esteem, respect, and conflict resolution, thus helping to prevent bullying. These efforts should extend to cyberbullying. It is important that family's concerns not be ignored and that counselors are available to meet with students and families and to refer them to other community resources when necessary.

Security measures should be explained to families. When family members understand that school security procedures help protect their children, they are more likely to comply and encourage others to participate. For example, many schools require families to sign in and get a name tag at the office before visiting classrooms. Some schools also have requirements for criminal checks for family members who want to volunteer.

At some schools, families have become actively involved in school safety. "Security Dads" began at Arlington High School in Indianapolis, Indiana, in 1991, and has now spread to other schools. These dads, who receive training and security checks, provide additional adult supervision at sports events, dances, and other extracurricular activities. They provide positive male role models and involve adult males at schools where females had previously done most of the volunteering. At Barnum Elementary School in Denver, Colorado, family and community members volunteer before and after school to keep an eye on children as they come and go. Before joining the brigade, parents receive training, a criminal background check, photo identification, and a bright green vest to wear. They are trained to not get involved themselves. Just serving as an extra set of eyes usually prevents problems, and when it doesn't, they use donated cell phones to call police.

Schools should establish a climate or school safety committee. Membership in such groups should include community members and family members in addition to the usual school staff members. A deliberate effort to include family and community members who represent culturally and linguistically diverse populations in the school should be made. A top priority for all families is their child's safety and well-being while on school grounds.

Families who are culturally and linguistically diverse may feel especially apprehensive about their children's safety if they are unfamiliar with the school procedures and routines. For example, family members may not understand why their kindergartner's classroom is located in an outside portable classroom and not inside the school's main building. Unsure of whom to ask about their concerns, they may send a family member to school each day at lunchtime to accompany the young students on their walk from the classroom to the cafeteria. This daily interest in safety may be regarded as a nuisance by school staff rather than as an act of loving concern. School security measures should be part of the school's welcome packet. Families should know to whom they can go with questions and concerns about their children's safety and to whom they should offer suggestions for improvement. Responsibility for establishing two-way communication with parents about school safety can be assigned to the school safety or climate committee. It is important that the information be available in multiple languages and that committee members speak the native languages of families or have translation services available. Family safety concerns should be welcomed at all times and followed up on by the committee and administration. Such concern and commitment on the part of the school builds a trusting relationship between the families and the school.

The topic of school safety should be systematically reviewed with the school staff along with the reminder to school staff to act upon parental/ family concerns. Such a review can occur at the beginning of each semester. School staff should remain vigilant about being culturally sensitive to families' concerns and not dismiss them as being unfounded or unimportant. When the staff takes time to carefully listen to concerns, ask questions, and seek input on solutions to problems, trust is built and sensitivity shown. Such interest must come from all school staff, including teachers, and not be regarded as outside anyone's job responsibilities or duties. Such actions make schools welcome and inviting places.

Families may also be interested in the safety and well-being of their children in the surrounding neighborhood outside the school grounds. Families at Robert Ford School in Lynn, Massachusetts, indicated that one of their top three priorities for the school was a safe and secure neighborhood. Because of this concern, the school reached out to the community and became a valuable resource to link services with families. (See websites for a related video and the school's website.)

Schools as Community Resources

There are many different ways of envisioning schools. Stakeholders such as teachers, administrators, children, and families may hold different ideas about what schools should be doing for children. One idea that most would agree on is that schools represent a tremendous investment of resources in communities. Schools have facilities, technology, literacy materials, faculty, and staff, which can be used to benefit communities in many ways. We would suggest that one way to meet the needs of the families of English language learners is to open these resources to the community. We have several suggestions about how schools can do this.

Schools have a number of facilities that are often underused. Traditionally, schools close at night. Lately, there has been a trend to keep schools open later and sometimes on weekends, usually for tutorials. If a school facility is seen as a resource, limiting the use of that resource to only part of the day is wasteful. Opening up school facilities to the families of children served by the school makes better use of that resource. It can create a much more open environment. Four areas that schools could open to families are the library, the nurse's office, the athletic fields and gyms, and the classrooms. Opening these underused facilities after school or even during the day can make the school a community center. (See other resources.)

Libraries

The school library can serve as a literacy center for the families of children in the school. School librarians should purchase books in the languages spoken by the family members and representing the cultures of families. (See websites.) Often, second language communities will have free newspapers in the languages spoken in the area. Having these available in the library will help family members feel comfortable in the library. If family members feel comfortable using the library, they are more likely to volunteer as book readers or shelving books. Schools in lower income areas may house more books than can be found in the homes of the children for an entire neighborhood. Many immigrant families are unfamiliar with school libraries in the United States. They sometimes think that they must pay to use the library, or they are afraid of the financial responsibility of having to replace a lost or damaged book. Library education and opening the library to families is a good way to improve both school climate and the literacy skills of the children in the school. Schools often serve neighborhoods where public community libraries are many miles away. Some schools have been able to keep their libraries open more hours by having staff on staggered schedules and by using community volunteers to fill in the gaps. If a school has one librarian and two assistants, one assistant could be on duty from 7 a.m. to 3 p.m. and another from 2 p.m. to 8 p.m. weekdays and 9 a.m. to 5 p.m. on Saturdays. The librarian could be there during normal school hours, and community volunteers could help in the evening and on Saturdays so no one would be alone. In Washington, D.C., the School Libraries Project renovated eight school libraries, which serve students during the day and the community in the evening. (See websites.)

School libraries might also wish to consider setting up a designated corner of the library for young families who have children not yet enrolled in school. This area would let younger siblings of students already enrolled in the school interact with books and become comfortable with the school setting and culture. The area can be stocked with donated books for infants and toddlers, and community volunteers can read during story times. Civic groups and faith-based organizations often look for service projects and may be a good source of donated books and volunteer readers. Additionally, libraries often weed out books that are no longer suitable for enrolled students but may be suitable for the reading corner. Schools uncomfortable with the idea of having young children present during school hours may wish to designate time before or after school for this purpose, because families often drop off and pick up children. Chapter 8 includes more information on partnering with civic organizations and groups for additional funds and donations. Rotary International is one organization that has an interest in promoting reading.

Nurses

According to the National Association for School Nurses, the school nurse serves as a liaison between school personnel, family, community, and health care providers. The nurse communicates with families through telephone calls, contacts them with written communication and home visits, and serves as a representative of the school community. The school nurse also communicates with community health providers and community health care agencies while ensuring appropriate confidentiality, develops community partnerships, and serves on community coalitions to promote the health of the community. (See websites.)

At Crawford Elementary School in Aurora, Colorado, a former kindergarten room serves as a school-based health clinic. Students at Crawford receive easy and low cost access to health care provided by the Rocky Mountain Youth Health Clinics, a nonprofit organization. Crawford Elementary makes it possible for students who may otherwise have little or no access to quality health care to receive much needed services with visits costing as little as two dollars. (See other resources.)

Seton Children's Hospital in Austin, Texas, provides the Skippy Mobile Health Clinic for children from infancy through age 18 in the Austin Independent School District. The clinic offers primary and preventive care to students at low cost and offers free immunizations for all children. Any school nurse in an Austin Independent School District school can put families in touch with services from the clinic. Lack of medical care that may once have led to student absences or impeded success in the classroom can be addressed through the mobile health clinic.

Health services are particularly important for children who live in poverty because they are more likely to suffer from physical and mental illnesses. More information about community health partnerships is available at the Center for Health and Health Care in Schools. (See websites.) This site is dedicated to helping schools and communities start school health centers. Schools should carefully explore the need to establish such services for all families in their community.

Athletic Facilities and Parks

Schools can become welcoming places to families by providing athletic facilities for the local community. Schools often have gymnasiums, basketball courts, and playing fields that can be used by children and families after school. Although supervision is always an issue, keeping these facilities closed during the after-school hours means that expensive facilities are not being used. This can be especially important in cities that have limited space for recreational activities.

At the beginning of the 20th century, the United States was experiencing the largest wave of immigration in its history. At the time, many Americans were afraid that the new immigrants were not assimilating into American society. Many lived in ethnic enclaves of Italians, Irish, Polish, Germans, or others. The parks and recreation movement that started around this time saw open spaces as opportunities to teach the new immigrant children English and to engage them in healthy activities away from the enclosed urban spaces. The same applies today.

Today, it is known that different ethnic groups use parks differently, and that immigrants tend to use nature parks less than white Americans. In addition, people have more health problems when they have less access to parks or natural spaces either because of fear of crime, discrimination, or lack of access. Schools can be a big part of increasing access to green space.

Families who participate in an after-school sports or recreation program are more likely to feel comfortable visiting the school with their children. Supervision of the programs can come through local Boys and Girls Clubs, scouting groups, or the United Way. Another source of supervision can come with a city-school partnership.

The city of Austin, Texas, maintains 16 parks in combination with school grounds. During the day, the parks are closed and the fields and playscapes are used by the school children. After school, the parks are open to the local community for recreation and sports programs. The city is responsible for the upkeep of the parks. Pasadena, California, also has a project where the schools and the city combine facilities. Currently, there are six city-school park partnerships. The city has provided funding to keep up parks and resurface the high school tennis courts in exchange for having these facilities open in the evenings, holidays, and on weekends.

Summer

For middle-class children, summer often means family vacations or summer camp, but for lower-income families, summer is not so idyllic. It is often a time without free school breakfast and lunch, a time trapped inside to avoid the dangers of the streets, and a time to look after younger siblings while parents work. Parents of all income levels worry about finding productive things for their children to do over the summer.

Summer is also the major reason for the achievement gap. Studies such as *The Learning Season: The Untapped Power of Summer to Advance Student Achievement* indicate that students from all income levels make similar progress during the school year, but students from lower income families have greater learning loss during the summer. (See websites.) More than half the achievement gap between lower and higher income youth can be attributed to summer. *Time Magazine* (July 22, 2010) said that by the end of elementary school, lower income youth have fallen almost three grade levels behind because of loss of learning over the summer. (See other resources.) According to Project Appleseed, more than 75 percent of elementary and middle school families want school-based summer programs, and 74 percent even said they would be willing to pay a fee. (See websites.) However, only 18 percent of the parents surveyed said their children attended a school-based summer program.

Year-round school programs have met resistance in many cities because of costs and opposition from teachers, higher-income families, and the tourist industry. Families of all incomes have trouble finding day care when school vacations are short and at times other than summer. Summer school is often offered only to failing students and provides more of the same type of instruction that was offered during the regular school year. Alternative summer programs are sprouting up across the country, especially to serve the needs of lower income students. In order to resolve funding and staffing problems, school districts partner with other public and private agencies and seek grants and funding available for summer programs serving low income youth. More information on these funding sources is available from the National Summer Learning Association. (See websites.) Although these programs differ, the most successful ones combine learning with the recreational aspects of summer camp. Because of the less formal nature of the learning and the involvement in the community, families feel more welcome at these programs and are more likely to become involved.

The 21st Century Redhound, a summer program organized by the Corbin, Kentucky, school district since 1991, is funded at the state and national levels as a 21st Century Community Learning Center. The school district partners with a wide variety of agencies, from Baptist Family Fitness to the Kentucky Fish and Wildlife Department. The summer program teaches all core areas through hands-on experiences and exploring the outdoors. Each week has a theme. Another summer program, Aim High, has served middle school youth in the San Francisco area since 1986. (See websites.) Students take academic classes and an adolescent development class in the morning. In the afternoons, they choose from art, sports, cultural activities, and other enrichment opportunities. Half the staff is bilingual, and the program especially seeks to serve English language learners and their families. Aim High is offered at multiple sites close to public transportation. Efforts to involve families include family orientation night, a family back-to-school night, weekly cultural days, and volunteer opportunities. The program also regularly seeks input and feedback from families.

After-School Programs

Eighty-two percent of parents would like their children to be involved in school-based after-school programs, but only 35 percent reported having that opportunity for their children, according to Project Appleseed. (See websites.) The vast majority of parents interested in after-school programs would like them to have computer and technology classes, art and music programs, and recreational activities. Most middle school parents would like their children to be involved in community service or volunteer opportunities.

Building Community

The families of English language learners often do not feel a part of the school community. At the high school level, sports, especially football, bring together many members of the community. They cheer the team on, sell sodas and snacks, and see old friends. However, families from other countries may not connect with football because it is primarily an American game. Therefore, other efforts may be necessary to bring families of English language learners into the school community. Schools can promote sports such as soccer, which is played around the world by both boys and girls. They can also do activities such as creating gardens, painting murals, or developing multicultural recipe books that may engage families that would not be involved in more traditional activities. (See websites.) Clubs that reflect the students' culture may also encourage students and families to become more involved in school. For example, Hispanic families may relate more to mariachi music or folklorico dancing than to some other activities.

Community Schools

Many schools across the country combine community services with educating students. Although the design differs from one community to the next, there are common threads. These community schools involve partnerships between school districts and other organizations, they provide social service programs to students and their families, and they have high levels of family engagement. In the past, the U.S. Department of Education funded only educational projects but, recognizing the importance of community partnerships for student success, it has begun to fund planning for community schools through its Promise Neighborhoods program.

The City Heights K–16 Educational Collaborative in San Diego, California, is an example of a school district partnering with community organizations to provide a variety of services for students and families. The collaborative has an elementary, middle, and high school in a neighborhood where 72,000 residents speak more than 30 languages. The facilities, which cover 30 acres, include housing, a continuing education center, a Head Start facility, a library, a swimming pool, tennis courts, a performance center, a community service center, sports fields, and a police station. This has encouraged high levels of family involvement in adult education, community service, and school governance meetings. (See websites.)

Ford School in Lynn, Massachusetts, is also a community school. Ford serves students in kindergarten thought eighth grade. Ninety-five percent of students get free or reduced lunch, and 57 percent of families speak limited English. The school's mission is to "dare to dream of a world in which all families will see the school as the center of the community, a resource for life-long learning, and a place where any parent, student, or neighbor can turn to find a helping hand and sympathetic ear." (See websites.) The school is open daily from 7 a.m. through 9 p.m. It partners with 12 different organizations, including community partners, businesses, higher education institutions, and NASA.

Principal Claire Crane first arrived at Ford in 1989. She interviewed school families and determined that parents' top three priorities were education, a safe and clean neighborhood, and day care. A unique feature that emerged as a result of the survey is Ford's night school, which offers twice-weekly classes taken by more than 250 parents and community members. Topics include English as a second language, GED test preparation, and citizenship. Homework help and evening care are provided for children while their families are taking classes. Ford is a strong example of a community school working to meet the needs of diverse families and communities. Schools interested in becoming a community school may want to review the website for the Coalition of Community Schools. (See websites.)

The John Spry Community School is located in La Villita (Little Village), an immigrant neighborhood of Chicago. (See websites.) The school serves neighborhood students in grades prekindergarten through 12 under one roof. The school is open year-round to support students six days a week, after hours, and throughout the summer. The high school located at the Spry Community School is called Community Links High School. Students can graduate in three years, and the school has a 100 percent graduation rate. The school requires students to complete internships with community involvement, such as working with a local hospital. High school students are also required to serve as tutors to elementary students. This tutoring is essential to the school since many of its elementary students are recent immigrants. Tutors serve as role models and speak the newcomers' native languages. Spry Community School also partners with the Boys and Girls Club to provide after-school programs for students and computer fundamentals and adult literacy for families and other adults in the community.

A good source of information about community schools is the National Center for Community Schools, operated by the Children's Aid Society of New York. (See websites.) The Children's Aid Society's operates 13 community schools in New York City in conjunction with the New York City Board of Education. The society pays for before- and after-school programs, health clinics, and parent rooms. One of the society's community schools is I.S. 218 in Washington Heights, a neighborhood in northern Manhattan. The school is open daily from 7 a.m. to 9 p.m. Special programs for students include a homework help session; activities such as a string ensemble and sports teams; comprehensive health services offered through a school-based health clinic; a parent room; and crisis counseling with social workers. Staff in the school speak multiple languages and are present to welcome and assist all families. A virtual school tour of I.S. 218 is available on the website. The site also provides specific information about how to begin a community school, numerous publications and resources, and case studies of successful community schools around the country.

Negative Practices

Some practices being used around the country to get parents more involved in schools are likely to turn families off, especially linguistically and culturally diverse families. One proposal in Florida is to have elementary school teachers grade the parents of the students in their class. Families contribute to the children's education in multiple ways, many of which go on in the home and are invisible to teachers and schools. Bad parent grades are likely to create more divisions between homes and schools rather than encouraging greater involvement.

Another negative practice is assuming parents need training to know what is best for their children. While many schools place a heavy emphasis on test scores from an early age, some families focus more on a safe and caring environment. Rather than telling families what they should want in a school, educators should listen to families' priorities, which will improve family engagement and, in turn, improve test scores.

Activity
Mystery Shopper

Purpose: This activity allows your school to measure the quality of the experience for first-time visitors to the school. Do the visitors have a warm and welcoming experience?

One of the great inventions of the fast-food world is the mystery shopper. The mystery shopper is someone who is paid to visit a restaurant at different times of the day to find out about the dining experience. They are employed by the owner or manager to find out how the customer sees the store. Is the store clean? Was the service polite and efficient? Was the food good? Try this at your own school by finding someone who has never been to your school before and asking them to visit.

Participants: A school administrator invites someone to come to the school posing as the parent of a child new to the neighborhood or as someone interested in volunteering at the school. It is best if the person speaks a language other than English.

Preparation and Resources: Hire someone as a "mystery shopper" and decide what they should look for. As few people as possible should know about this project in advance because you want to get an honest assessment of the school climate.

Description of Activity: The "mystery shopper" may look at different things on different campuses, but the following are some suggestions:

- ◆ Is signage clear and in the languages of the school community?
- ◆ How hard is it to navigate security?
- ◆ How hard is it to find the office?

- ◆ Are there bilingual/multilingual staff available in the office?
- ◆ How are visitors greeted when they come to the office?
- ◆ How are families greeted when students are brought to the school campus?
- ◆ Do school staff members greet students and families by name?
- ◆ What is posted on the walls of the school? Are there student work displays and lists of upcoming school and community events?
- ◆ What interactions occur between teachers and parents or family members?
- ◆ Does the school treat parents who do not speak English differently from English-speaking parents?

Share the findings with all stakeholders and discuss areas of strength and areas needing improvement.

Options: Have different "mystery shoppers" and compare how the school treats parents who speak English and those who don't; how men are treated compared to women; how professionally dressed people are treated compared to people dressed for manual labor.

Another potential mystery shopper activity is to have a parent or family member try to schedule a meeting with a faculty member or an administrator.

Activity
New Teacher Induction/Community Travel

Purpose: Identify cultural assets within the community to support schools. This activity is based on suggestions made in the article, "A Place for All Families," by Ramirez and Soto-Hindman (2009).

Participants: New teachers and staff

Preparation and Resources: Map of the community that outlines the school attendance zone; form of transportation: walking, cars, or buses; and paper and pencil for taking notes.

Description of Activity: On three different occasions throughout the school year, travel two or three miles out into the community using the school as a starting point. Take a different route each time you visit the community. Analyze what students pass each day on their way to and from school. Note the types of homes students live in, the shops and businesses located on the route, languages spoken and seen in print, medical facilities, childcare facilities, community agencies, parks or recreational opportunities, places of worship, libraries, and general landmarks and landscapes that the students pass.

After completing the community travel, teachers record observations and discuss with the faculty what they have observed and noted. The discussion should center on the assets of the community rather than a negative discussion of what the community does not have. Principals, veteran staff members, or a parent-community liaison can take turns leading the discussion. Questions may arise from the debriefing/discussion sessions. They may be collected and posed to parents and community members. School staff should be encouraged to examine stereotypes they may have held about their communities prior to the community trips.

Community trip discussions may be extended to a brainstorming session about how the community can be better utilized to engage all families. Such ideas may include exploring the potential of contacting places of worship and local businesses to be community partners to help communicate school events and information. For example, a local hair or nail salon could have copies of the school newsletter available for families to read in their native language. Copies of children's books in native languages might also be available for children to read and look at while children wait for family members. Local grocery stores may have fliers in students' native language advertising weekly specials. Such fliers may be utilized in a family literacy activity that teaches concepts about print.

Options: A variation on this activity would be to include all school personnel, including veteran teachers, bus drivers, cafeteria workers, office staff, paraprofessionals, and security guards on community trips and the resulting discussions of community assets that can be used to support the school.

Activity
School Safety Survey

Purpose: School safety is a high priority for all families. Educators are often not aware of the perceptions of the school in the community. Although the school itself may appear safe, walking to and from school or taking the bus may present security problems. That is why it is important to find out the perceptions of school safety from all those involved, including culturally and linguistically diverse families.

Participants: Families

Preparation and Resources: Plans to gather information. Written surveys in the languages spoken by the families in the community may be a starting point but additional meetings out in the community may be necessary to gather information from diverse families. Prepare responses to concerns that are raised during this process.

Description of Activity: Questions will vary from campus to campus but suggestions include:

- ◆ Does your child feel safe in school? If not, when does your child feel he or she is in danger? (For example, some students feel secure in class but are taunted on the playground.)
- ◆ Does your child feel safe going to and from school? If not, what makes your child feel insecure?
- ◆ Is your child bullied at school? If so, when?
- ◆ Have you ever contacted the school about a safety concern? What was that concern? How was it handled?

After information has been collected, it should be reviewed and plans made to address concerns. Family members should be informed of the steps being taken.

Options: Staff members may want to discuss topics related to safety at a meeting. The staff might consider questions like these:

- ◆ Do you feel safe at the school? If not, what concerns you?
- ◆ Is there a school climate or safety committee?
- ◆ Are families and community members a part of the committee?
- ◆ What does this committee do and how often does it meet?
- ◆ What process is used when family members have safety concerns? How long does this take?
- ◆ How and in what languages are school safety measures communicated to families?
- ◆ What changes have been made at your campus based on community or family input related to safety issues?

Resources

Multicultural Books

Becoming Naomi León, by Pam Muñoz Ryan (2005), is a chapter book about the experiences of a girl living with her great-grandmother and younger brother in the United States. Her mother is from the United States, while her father is from Mexico. She doesn't know either parent well. When Naomi's mother returns to take her away from her great-grandmother, the family flees to Mexico to find her father. In Oaxaca, Naomi begins to learn about the culture of her father and is finally reunited with him. When she returns to the United States, she realizes how her experiences have changed her from a mouse to a lion.

Sitti's Secrets, by Naomi Shihab Nye (1994), is a picture book that describes the life of a girl of Palestinian descent who lives in the United States with her family. The book describes her visit to her grandmother living in Palestine. She is unable to speak to her grandmother, so her father translates for her. Although they cannot communicate verbally, they spend time together sharing her grandmothers' activities like baking flatbread and making lemonade using the lemons from her grandmother's tree. The emphasis of the story is that although people do different things and eat different foods, they have much in common.

A Step from Heaven, by An Na (2003), describes the life of a girl, Young Ju, who is born in Korea and who moves to the United States with her family as a young girl. As she gets older, she learns more about the struggles of her family in adapting to American culture, which does not have the same values as her parents. As Young Ju grows older, she begins to adapt to American ways, which upsets her family. Eventually, the stress of living in the United States becomes too much for her father, and he returns to Korea. Young Ju is left alone in the United States with her mother. The story challenges the stereotype that families from Asian descent easily assimilate in the United States and become successful, yet affirms that people can be resilient when making choices between two cultures.

Websites
Aim High Summer School Program
www.aimhigh.org

> Aim High is a nonprofit organization that operates an intensive five-week summer school program for middle school students in the San Francisco Bay area. The site covers the five key components of the program, including parent/caregiver involvement and partnership with the community.

Coalition for Community Schools
www.communityschools.org

> This website contains extensive information about community schools, including national models, resources, and publications.

Community School Video and Website
www.jsonline.com/general/37714089.html?bcpid=8725036001&bctid=53499150001

> Video featuring the principal of Robert L. Ford School in Lynn, Massachusetts, and its designation as a community school. http://ford.lynnschools.org is the school website.

Educational Collaborative

http://thechec.org

> This website explains the City Heights Educational Collaborative in San Diego, California. The community-school collaborative provides health and social services to students and families.

Health in Schools

www.healthinschools.org

> The Center for Health and Health Care in Schools is a resource center operated from George Washington University's School of Public Health and Health Services. The center describes its mission as working to strengthen and improve the well-being of children and youth through effective health programs and health care services in schools. The site contains tools, model programs, and resources. Of particular interest is the center's project for immigrant and refugee children, which is focused on reducing their emotional and behavioral health problems through community partnerships. The website contains information for educators, parents, and health professionals interested in building school-based health programs.

Kids Gardening

www.kidsgardening.org/school-gardening

> School Gardening is a section of the Kids Gardening website operated by the National Gardening Association. It is devoted to how to get started, teacher lessons and links, and professional development.

Multicultural Literature

www.education.wisc.edu/ccbc/books/detaillistbooks.asp?idbooklists=42

> The Cooperative Children's Book Center from the School of Education at the University of Wisconsin at Madison offers a website with a list of *50 Multicultural Books That Every Child Should Know* for preschoolers through age 12. The books are grouped by age and include a review of each book. The site also provides a link to *30 Multicultural Books That Teens Should Know,* www.education.wisc.edu/ccbc/books/detailListBooks.asp?idBookLists=253

National Association of School Nurses

www.nasn.org/Default.aspx?tabid=279

> This website is a comprehensive source of information for school nurses. The site describes itself as the leading worldwide expert for school health issues. It links school nurses to various health and wellness resources. The site also contains a link to each state's affiliate website, for example, the Texas School Nurses Organization, the School Nurses Organization of Arizona, and the New York Association of School Nurses.

National Center for Community Schools

http://nationalcenterforcommunityschools.childrensaidsociety.org

> This website provides information about how to start community schools and provides documents and tools, a virtual school site visit and newsletter based on the experience of the Children's Aid Society's community schools in New York City.

Parent Friendliness Training

Advocates for Children of New York. *Our Children, Our Schools: A Blueprint for Creating Partnerships Between Immigrant Families and New York City Public Schools.* Retrieved from www.advocatesforchildren.org/Our_Children_Our_Schools%20 _FINALReport.pdf

> This publication, by Advocates for Children of New York, was compiled based on interviews done with more than 80 immigrant parents and community representatives about barriers to participation in New York City Schools. The report includes recommendations and promising practices to help promote successful partnerships between schools and immigrant families. A wide variety of cultures are represented in the publication, including Asian, Pacific Islander, Caribbean, Eastern European, Latin American, Middle Eastern, North African and South Asian communities.

Project Appleseed

www.projectappleseed.org/barriers.html

> This portion of the Project Appleseed website presents research on barriers to parental involvement in schools. Project Appleseed is an organization devoted to public school reform, especially through parental involvement. The site contains an extensive list of resources on family events, engagement, research, and student success topics (homework, school reform, standardized testing, health and wellness information for families) as well as numerous links to educational organizations.

School Libraries Project

www.schoollibrariesproject.org

> The School Libraries Project website presents information on the community renovation of eight public school libraries in the Capitol Hill Neighborhood of Washington D. C. The libraries were renovated through a partnership of community members and the school to create spaces that promoted reading and inspired children. The website includes videos of the transformation of each of the eight libraries; descriptions of the mission and goals related to the project; facility designs utilized; community partners (architects, universities, and volunteers) and a detailed description of the budget required to carry out the project.

Spry Community School

A video about Spry Community School entitled "Around the Clock Learning: an Extended Definition" may be viewed at www.youtube.com/watch?v= 9OWqVv7WAZo. John Spry Community Elementary School's website is found at www.spry.cps.k12.il.us and the Community Links High School website is found at www.comlinkshs.org.

Summer Learning

www.summerlearning.org

> Home page for the National Summer Learning Organization. This site contains publications, resources, and ideas to support summer learning programs for all children.

Summer School Benefits

http://nmefdn.net/uploads/Learning_Season_ES.pdf

> *The learning season: The untapped power of summer to advance student achievement* is a research report published by the Nellie Mae Foundation highlighting the benefits gained from summer learning along with policy and research recommendations for schools and communities.

Other Resources

Allen, J. (September 2, 2010). More schools use school-based, mobile health clinics.

Public Health Law & Policy (2010). *Opening school grounds to the community after hours: A toolkit for increasing physical activity through joint use agreements.* Retrieved from www.phlpnet.org/system/files/Joint_Use_Toolkit_FINAL_web _2010.01.28.pdf

Ramirez, A. Y. & Soto-Hinman, I. (2009). A place for all families. *Educational Leadership.* 66(7), pp. 79–82.

Tucker, J. (March 21, 2007) San Francisco: Safety is priority for parents shopping for public schools. *San Francisco Chronicle.* Retrieved from http://articles.sfgate .com/2007-03-21/bay-area/17236511_1_school-safety-children-in-private -schools-safe-school Retrieved from http://articles.sfgate.com/2007-03-21/bay -area/17236511_1_school-safety-children-in-private-schools-safe-school

Von Drehle, D. (July 22, 2010) The case against summer vacation. *Time Magazine.*

Washoe County School District. *Family friendly schools guide* (English). Retrieved from www.washoe.k12.nv.us/docs/pdf/FamilyFriendlyGuide-WebsiteSept061.pdf

Washoe County School District. *Family friendly schools guide* (Spanish). Retrieved from http://www.washoe.k12.nv.us/docs/pdf/FamilyFriendlyGuideSpanish -Website06-07.pdf

Wisconsin Department of Public Instruction. *Organizing a successful family center in your school: A resource guide.* Retrieved from http://dpi.state.wi.us/fscp/pdf/fcsprntc.pdf

Wong, H. K. (2005). New teacher induction: The foundation for comprehensive, coherent and sustained professional development. In Portner, H. (Ed.). *Teacher mentoring and induction: The state of the art and beyond* (pp. 41–58). Thousand Oaks, CA: Corwin Press.

4

Beyond Open Houses

Ricardo's teacher was having a family meeting tonight from 7 to 8 p.m. Ricardo's mom, Patricia, always looked forward to these meetings, which gave her time to have dinner with her children and still get them to bed at a reasonable hour after the meeting. Best of all, the teacher encouraged her to bring Ricardo and his younger sister, Marisa, with her. When they arrived in the first-grade classroom, the desks had been moved to the side and adult-sized folding chairs had been placed in a semicircle. In front of the chairs was a large rug area. Ms. Sandoval greeted everyone and then encouraged the children to sit on the rug and the adults to sit on the chairs, grouped by language. She used a big book in English to demonstrate how to do a read-aloud, beginning by looking at the cover and title and making predictions about what the story would be about. Then she read and showed the pictures to the children on the rug, making sure to stop and point out important points but not stop so often they would lose the story line.

After she finished reading, she asked the children if the book reminded them of anything in their lives. A parent who spoke English and Spanish and a parent who spoke English and Somali volunteered to paraphrase important points to the parents who did not speak English and translate their comments or questions. Ms. Sandoval also explained how to make up stories to go with a picture book if the child brought home a book in English that no one at home could read.

Then everyone helped Ms. Sandoval move the chairs into a circle with the chairs facing outward and put a number on each chair. In the meantime, she placed a variety of picture books in English, Spanish, and Somali out on a table at the side of the room. Family members and students walked around the outside of the circle of chairs to the music. When the music stopped, Ricardo would find a seat and Ms. Sandoval would pull two numbers out of a jar. The students on the chairs with those numbers got to choose a book from the table to take home. Chairs and numbers were removed until there were only four students and their families walking around the circle. Ms. Sandoval made sure there were enough books for all the students in her class as well as their siblings who had come to the meeting. Ms. Sandoval pointed out the sign-up sheet for conferences on her desk and encouraged families who wanted to learn about the progress of their child to sign up for an individual confidential conference. Patricia signed up for a Sunday afternoon conference with the teacher. As families left, Ms. Sandoval handed out tips to reading aloud to your child in English, Spanish, and Somali.

Ms. Sandoval's meeting engaged families of English language learners in many ways. Instead of just telling families how to do a read-aloud, she demonstrated it and included the children in the discussion. The session was targeted for families of first graders but she made sure to include siblings in the activities. Translators paraphrased important points rather than translating word for word, which is time-consuming. Each family went home with books and a tip sheet in their native language. She also kept the meeting short so that it would not disrupt the family schedule too much.

Although traditional open houses are well-meaning, they often fall short in a number of ways. They tend to focus on the school providing information rather than interacting with families. The same information is often provided throughout the year and to families with children at all different grade levels. Famlies may go home emptyhanded rather than with ideas they can implement. There are many ways of making family meetings more engaging for everyone, especially the families of English language learners.

- ◆ Ask families what they would like to do at these meetings.
- ◆ Offer family sessions at different times and different days.
- ◆ Invite families with notes in their home language.
- ◆ Make sure the meeting is interactive. Families should not just be passive listeners.
- ◆ Avoid simultaneous translation.
- ◆ Provide information or materials that families can use at home.
- ◆ Have sign-up sheets for families who want to speak with the teacher individually about their child.
- ◆ Respect families who do not come to school.

What Families Want

Different families need and want different things from the school. (See Chapter 2.) In addition, the families of children in first grade may have very different needs or wants from those with children in fifth grade. Families may prefer certain types of sessions at the beginning of the year and other types toward the end of the year. Despite the desire of teachers and administrators to have sessions that attract the most families at the same time, it may be necessary to have more frequent, smaller, targeted meetings.

Schools can organize a variety of events, such as carnivals, movie nights, or gardening events that appeal to families. Outside organizations may sponsor health fairs, crime prevention programs, pet care workshops, continuing education courses, or after-school tutoring. Even though some of these activities do not relate directly to student learning, they help to build a learning community and encourage a greater variety of families to come to school and feel comfortable in the school setting.

Since time, money, and other resources are limited, it is important to reflect on the purpose of events and whether the event that your school is having will meet your objectives. For example, perhaps the purpose of the event is to get families reading more at home with their children. You have someone read a big book to the children and parents with great expression. Afterwards families and children do an art activity related to the book and share them. There was a good turnout, everyone seemed excited by the book reading and activities, and they went home with their art projects. In speaking with families later, you find out that they were really excited by the program, but they don't have access to children's books. Books checked out of the school library are supposed to be kept in desks at school, and the public library is on the other side of town. In addition, most of the books in both the school and public library are in English. Although the event itself was very successful, the objective was not met. Here are some questions to consider when planning an event:

- ◆ Why are we having this event?
- ◆ What are we doing to make sure the purpose of the event is met?
- ◆ What may be some obstacles to our objectives? How can we overcome them?
- ◆ What are we doing to involve as many families as possible, including families of English language learners?
- ◆ How will we know if the event is successful and the objectives were met?

When

There is no good time for everyone, although there are probably some times that should be avoided. For example, in some communities, there are many church activities on Wednesday nights. Schools should try different times, including scheduling activities during the day, evenings, and weekends to allow most families an opportunity to participate in at least some of the activities. Not all family members will work 8 to 5 during the week so accomodations need to be made for those who work night or weekend shifts.

Notes

Invitations to the events should be written in the home language spoken by families. A calendar of events allows families to plan in advance but should be followed up with a reminder. If possible, address the notes to the family and have the student participate in writing or illustrating the note. More tips on writing notes home are given in Chapter 5.

Interactive Meetings

Family meetings are often thought of as a time when administrators and teachers provide information to families, but this type of session can be boring and does not engage families. The ideas that are provided in this chapter involve families, including children, in activities that go beyond question-and-answer sessions. As teachers and administrators participate in activities with families, they will learn more about the families' knowledge and their contributions to the success of their children. Once you begin to think of family meetings in this way, you will probably have many more ideas than are provided in this chapter.

Translation

There is nothing less engaging than someone providing information in English and then having someone immediately translate it into another language. If a large number of families speak the same language, then it is best to provide a session in that language in a separate room from the English session. However, the person presenting in the other language must have deep knowledge of both the content and the language in order to conduct the session. Many times people will have conversational knowledge of a language but have difficulty with more technical concepts. Sometimes it is best to videotape the original presentation in English and then allow the translator time to study it before translating it for an audience at a later date. If a small number of families speak a specific language, group the families together for the session and place someone who can translate near the group. The translator can present the major ideas during the English session and then go into more detail as the families engage in the activities.

Materials

Families should go home with materials or at least a list of ideas of things they can do at home. In addition, they should be provided with telephone numbers, addresses, and websites where more information and materials can be obtained at little or no cost.

Individual Conferences

Many families come to school meetings wanting to know more about the progress of their individual child. Explain to families the purpose of the meeting that they are attending and that it is not possible to speak privately with each family at this time but have a sign-up sheet with a variety of times for individual conferences with families. These sign-up sheets should even be available during family movie nights or school carnivals so that families who normally don't come to school can be contacted at this time.

Respect

Despite extensive efforts by the school to involve diverse families, some families still will not be able to attend because of work schedules, sick relatives, lack of transportation, or other issues. If the school is able to get a grant or other funding, it may want to arrange transportation for families to school. Sometimes arrangements can be made for special tickets on public transportation. Nevertheless, some families will not attend meetings at school. This should not be mistaken as indifference or poor parenting because most likely these families also want their children to receive a good education but simply cannot make it to school.

Beyond Open House

Although it is easier to have a few meetings that target all families, this will result in engaging fewer families. A variety of events should be spread out during the year and focus on different ages, cultures, and interests of students and their families. For planning purposes, these can be thought of as events in four categories: classroom events, targeted events, schools events, and events held in conjunction with other organizations in the community.

Classroom Events

Classroom events should target the specific needs that families identify. They may differ depending on the time of the year and on the families participating. One example of this type of event is the "house meeting," which is used in Los Angeles (Auerbach, 2009). Classroom teachers in Los Angeles lead monthly one-hour discussions in their classrooms rather than having traditional meetings such as open houses and parent teacher association meetings. Examples of topics for these meetings include why education is important, how to help children at home, or free things to do with children. Through family story sharing, teachers learn more about the families they serve, families are empowered, and they learn from each other. Often families form bonds that continue outside of the monthly meetings. The "house meetings" in Los Angeles have been especially successful in building relationships with culturally and linguistically diverse families who might otherwise be hesitant to approach the school and share concerns or ask questions. This strategy can start with a few volunteer teachers and spread to the rest of the school after strategies are practiced and challenges resolved with a few classes.

Teachers at one grade level may also want to get together to sponsor appropriate activities. By having different grade level family nights on different nights, families who have children in two or more grades can attend sessions for all their children. Many of the activities at the end of the chapter would be appropriate to do as a grade level. For example, families often want to know more about standardized testing, and the content and reporting of these tests vary from grade to grade.

Targeted Events

Some information is more pertinent to certain families than others. For example, families of English language learners often need to decide whether their children will be in bilingual, dual language, English as a second language, or all English classes. Special sessions for families of incoming kindergarteners and new families may be held before families sign the papers placing their children in a program. It is important that families understand the strengths and weaknesses of each of the choices that are available and are able to ask questions in their native language. In our experience, most families of English language learners want their children to learn English as quickly as possible. They may not choose a bilingual or English as a second language program even when it is available because they don't understand the support their children may need while making the transition from their native language to English. The purpose of the sessions should not be to coerce families into making a specific decision but to help them understand the options available at the school. Other sessions may be held for families of English language learners in the different types of programs at your school as they progress through the grades. Families often have many questions about assessments in the native language and in English, exiting bilingual or English as a second language programs, how they can help their children at home if they can't speak English, how they can get their children extra help in learning English, and many other questions that are specific to families of English language learners. They are unlikely to ask these questions or find the answers if they are only invited to attend general open houses with families who speak English as their native language. Some English language learners are also in other special programs, including gifted and talented programs, Saturday tutoring programs, or programs for learning disabled students. Targeted events may be held for families who have children in these programs and arrangements should be made to have translators available or sessions in different rooms for those who speak only languages other than English. Questions or concerns about these programs may not surface in general meetings with other families, which is why targeted events are important.

The parent teacher organization has information on reaching out to multicultural and immigrant families. (See websites.) The PTA at Hollifield Station Elementary School in Maryland sponsored an American culture night with help from the district's English for speakers of other languages and family outreach specialists. The families rotated from station to station with an intepreter who spoke their home language. Topics included holidays and celebrations, school policies, classroom culture, athletics and competitions, and parent teacher conferences. At the end, the interpreters led the families through mock teacher-parent conferences, explaining the expectations of the teachers. Young-chan Han, the family outreach specialist, said that in some cultures families are discouraged from helping with homework or becoming involved in their children's education, so American expectations must be explicitly explained or demonstrated to them. In addition to providing targeted information for immigrant families, American culture night has child care available so that families are not discouraged from coming because they cannot find child care.

Other targeted events are recommended in the activities at the end of the chapter, including sessions about making the transition to high school and making transitions to higher education and jobs after high school.

Schoolwide Events

There are many types of schoolwide events that help develop positive feelings about the school and may attract families that would not come to more traditional meetings or even sporting events, such as football. The PTA provides information and applications for free kits to put on go green nights, family reading nights, movie nights, and family game nights. (See websites). The free planning kit for the go green nights has ideas for family nights that include energy saving tips and science experiments. The kit for the family reading nights provides creative ideas to get families reading together. The movie night's kit explains how to get a license to show movies at school and ways to attract more families to those events. The game night's kit has ideas to get everyone up and moving. Many other ideas are available online from school districts. (See websites.)

Vine Hill Elementary School in Scotts Valley, California, has what they call "Family Fun Nights" twice a year. (See websites.) These events have included movie nights, ice cream social and science fun, pancakes for dinner night, bingo night, and craft nights. Some of the nights such as "Fiesta de Vine Hill" attracted families of English language learners of Mexican descent and others with Mexican crafts, music, dancing, and snacks. The family nights are free and open to everyone. The only rule is that children must be accompanied by adults. Venues outside the school, such as the Scotts Valley Community Center, also help attract families that may not feel comfortable coming to school. Teachers and other school staff can bring their families and mingle with students' families in a less formal setting.

Another example of nontraditional schoolwide events is gardening. More than a thousand schools around the country have gardens that involve students, teachers, families, and other community members. The National Gardening Association has a website devoted to ideas for school gardens and information about funding opportunities. (See websites.) Families can be involved in planning gardens, preparing an area for planting, weeding, maintaining, and participating in garden extension activities. Schools have many varieties of gardens, including flower gardens, herb gardens, vegetable gardens, butterfly gardens, and small window box gardens.

Wright Middle School, a school with 22 percent English language learners in Nashville, Tennessee, won a national award for its peace garden. (See websites.) The garden was established and is run by the Healthy School Team, a partnership of teachers, staff, parents, and community members. The plants reflect many of the 40 different countries represented by the students at the middle school. Signs are being placed in the garden to show locations around the world where the plants originated. This garden helps show students and their families that their culture is valued too.

Community-School Partnership Events

With community-school partnerships, resources needed to put on an event and involve families are shared. Many organizations are eager to reach out to more families in the community. The partnerships take many different forms. For example, orchestras, zoos, or nature centers may offer free or low-cost admission to families from a specific school on special designated days. Or community organizations may sponsor special programs at the school, such as health fairs or pet care days. These may be one-day events or ongoing partnerships.

At Peachtree Ridge High School in Suwanee, Georgia, the Gwinnett County District Attorney's office, the Gwinnett Police Department, and the school police teamed up to do a presentation and question-and-answer session for families. They spoke about the safe use of technology and potential dangers students and parents face in the use of cell phones, chat rooms, video cams, social media, and gaming systems. They highlighted the latest ways to safeguard yourself and your personal information.

The National Museum of Mexican Art partners with a Chicago Public School each year to participante in a Dia de los Muertos exhibition. (See websites.) Students, teachers, and parents work with museum staff to create an ofrenda or installation to be displayed at the museum. In addition to preparing for this one day event, the art museum partners with the Chicago Public Schools Bilingual Parent Resource Center to provide ongoing after-school programs at three Chicago schools.

The following are more ideas for family engagement events. Not all activities will be appropriate for all cultures. For example, the activity about jump rope songs would not be appropriate when dealing with cultures that do not jump rope. Other families may participate but without providing their own examples of songs or chants.

Activity
Jump Rope Songs

Purpose: Families are encouraged to share jump rope songs and chants from their childhood in their native language. This simple activity validates family knowledge and helps strengthen connections between home and school cultures. For teachers, it is an opportunity to learn more about families and to view family members as sources of information rather than as people who need to be "educated." Families from Mexico may also be familiar with traditional *rondas*, which are movement activities to music that are taught in the Mexican curriculum.

Participants: Families with children and teachers

Preparation and Resources: Although this activity is appropriate for kindergarten through fifth grade, schools may want to try it with one grade level at a time so that the numbers do not become overwhelming. All the preparation that is needed is an invitation to families and gathering the necessary resources—long jump ropes, one or two jump rope songs or chants, access to a gymnasium or a safe outdoor area, and water.

Description of Activity: The family activity facilitator explains the importance of spending time with children, developing their oral language, and exercising. The facilitator tells families that they will be doing jump rope chants today and encourages families to share jump rope songs or chants that they remember from their own childhood in their native language. If families are having trouble getting started, the facilitator should share one song. Then divide the whole group up into smaller groups of six to eight, give each group a long jump rope, and have fun. (Remember, two people at a time will be needed to spin the rope.)

Options: For younger children, the rope may be held still slightly off the ground and the children may jump back and forth over the stationary rope. Jump rope songs and chants from families can be collected, printed up, and sent home at a later date. This should not be done in advance because families may think they have to limit themselves to the songs and chants that have been printed. Bring marbles, jacks, sidewalk chalk, balls and other items so families can share other outdoor games they play. Find family members who are familiar with traditional rondas and are willing to teach one or two simple ones to students, teachers, and families. Make sure to have appropriate music on hand.

Activity
Grocery Store Flyers

Purpose: Educators can demonstrate different activities to do with free grocery store flyers during the school meeting and provide a list of activities that can be done at home. The flyers can be used for activities to increase oral language development, reading, health, and math skills.The flyers are given out free to advertise sales at the grocery store. Educators can ask to receive the extras for a few weeks so they can use them for family events. If the school serves a specific neighborhood, it is best to get the flyers from a neighborhood grocery store. Although grocery store flyer activites are free and easy to do, they vary with grade level, so it is best to conduct separate meetings for various levels of children.

Participants: Families with children and teachers

Preparation and Resources: Collect enough grocery store sale flyers for all the familes expected to attend the event. Send out invitations in families' home language if possible. If children of various grade levels will be present in one evening, you may want to have different rooms available so that the families can be divided by grade level. One of the activities also requires having food group charts available for the families. Others require plain paper, scissors, and glue.

Description of Activity: Grocery store flyers can be used as the basis for many different activities depending on the level of the students. Some activities would be appropriate at many grade levels while others might require the children to already have certain skills.

- ◆ Pre-K–6: Encourage families to discuss the items in the grocery store flyer with their children in their native language. They can discuss when the food would be eaten, how it would be prepared, and what else the children like to eat with that food.
- ◆ Pre-K–1: Encourage families to cut out and paste down items that they would like for breakfast, lunch, dinner, and snacks.
- ◆ 2–6: Provide families with a copy of the food pyramid and explain each level. Have families find items in the flyer that would go in each category of the food pyramid. They could cut and paste them into categories, write them down, or just discuss them.
- ◆ 2–6: Encourage families to find the most expensive items in the flyer. In their native language, encourage families to discuss what types of items are most expensive. Have families find the least expensive items in the flyer. What types of items are they?
- ◆ 3–8: Encouarge families to select items they would like to eat and add up the cost of the items. For a more challenging activity, talk about how many pounds of meat, vegetables, or fruit might be needed to feed their family and have them multiply the per pound price by the number of pounds needed and then add the costs together.
- ◆ 3–8: Have families pretend they have $50 to spend on food from the flyer. What would be the healthiest choices that would add up to no more than $50?
- ◆ 4–8: Look at the sale prices. What is the difference between the sale price and the regular price? What percentage discount is this?

Options: Ask families what ideas they have for using the grocery store flyer with their children. This will help families think of activities they can do at home.

Activity
Book Writing

Purpose: Families and their children can write and illustrate their own books. The books can then be taken home and shared with other family members and read over and over again.

Participants: Families and students of all ages, facilitator

Preparation and Resources: Invitations to the event should be sent in home languages. Plenty of materials should be gathered for the event, including paper, pens or pencils, crayons, markers, colored pencils, folders with prongs, and paper protectors.

Description of Activity: Provide a broad prompt to older family members such as "my childhood" and then brainstorm ideas that family members could put in their books. Provide paper for the pages to the adult family members. Family members then write at the bottom of each page. As they finish writing on a page, it is passed to students for illustration. After the book is finished, provide families with plastic page protectors and have them place the pages in the sheets back to back. After all the pages are in the protectors, have the families put them in a folder with prongs. Use markers to write the title, author, and illustrator on the cover of the folder.

Options: Instead of providing a prompt and then brainstorming, use a book or poem, such as Judith Viorst's "If I Were in Charge of the World," to help family members begin writing. Older students can write and illustrate their own books for their family at the same time the family member is writing a book for the student. Book topics can relate to family themes, favorite things, holidays, alphabet books, and counting books to name a few. In addition to crayons and markers, books can be illustrated with photographs, clip art, paint, or potato prints. There are many inexpensive ways to make books with children including accordion books, stick and elastic books, scroll books, and step books. (See websites.)

Activity
Standardized Testing

Purpose: Standardized testing has become more common at all grade levels across the country and has greater impact on children and their families than ever before. One state report for parents includes scale scores, confidence intervals, and some item analysis. All of this information is not very helpful if family members do not understand the information. It is even more difficult for non-English readers when this information comes only in English. Tests for reading diagnostics for young children can also be very confusing. The Texas Primary Reading Inventory (TPRI) and the Dynamic Indicators of Basic Early Literacy Skills (DIBELS) among other assessments of early reading have terminology that many parents will not be familiar with. Phonological awareness, phonemic awareness, and fluency are three common areas of assessment with which most parents will have no experience.

Families want to know what is assessed, how it is assessed, how they can help their children do better on the assessment, how to interpret the scores, and what impact the scores will have on their children's future. Many families get information about standardized testing through word of mouth, which is not always reliable. Planning a parent night around standardized assessments helps make families a better part of the instructional process. For non-English speaking families, this can be especially important. Few Spanish-speaking countries use any type of early assessment and rarely use the type of standardized assessments found in the United States. For families who use non-alphabetic languages like Mandarin Chinese, Korean, or Arabic, these assessments are even more problematic.

Participants: Families and educators who can explain assessments clearly in the languages needed.

Preparation and Resources: Varies with the activities chosen.

Description of Activity: Explain how to read test scores. Most schools give different assessments at different grade levels so separate sessions should be conducted for families of children taking each of the different assessments. Provide examples of pretend test scores projected on a screen. Explain what each score means and allow families to ask questions. Then explain the significance of each score. For example, a 70 percent on a norm referenced test is different than a 70 percent on a criterion referenced test and this may need to be explained to families. Families should also learn what happens when children do exceptionally well or poorly on the assessment. Will children be recommended for more diagnostic testing when they receive certain scores? What assistance does the school provide to students who score poorly on the assessment?

Soon after explaining the scoring system to a large group of families, educators should meet individually with families who want to review their child's last test score. These conferences need to be confidential, conducted away from other families, and conducted in the families' dominant language. Many times families receive scores but do not know how these scores compare to others at the same grade level or what the scores mean in terms of the child's future. Since standardized tests are often used to make decisions about retention and special needs programs, it is important that families know how to interpret the scores. These conferences could be set up at the same time as families go from station to station in other activities or sign-up sheets could be provided for conferences at a later date.

Families can go from station to station to learn about the different components of the tests and what they can do at home to assist their children. Even if the child is being tested in English, families should be provided with ideas of things they can do at home in their native language. For example, the child might read something in English but a family member could ask questions in their native language to get the child to discuss what they read. Although a family member may not be able to read word problems in English, they probably can help the child with basic mathematical processes, such as multiplication and division, in their native language. It is very important that all family members leave believing they can help their child at home no matter what their academic or English skills are.

Activity
High School Preparation

Purpose: When families understand and participate in course selection, better choices are made and students have greater academic achievement. Especially in large high schools, students may not understand the long-term consequences of their choices and simply choose classes that are easiest or that their friends are attending.

Participants: Middle school students and their families, high school counselors, trained volunteers

Preparation and Resources: Invitations should be sent home in the appropriate home languages. Arrangements should be made to have the high school counselors and volunteers come to the middle school. The event requires one large room and several small rooms or cubicles where families can receive individual counseling after the general session.

Description of Activity: Families with students who will attend high school the following year sign up for conferences either immediately after the session or on another day. A high school counselor or other expert discusses the transition from middle school to high school. The counselor discusses issues such as course and program choices. Some high schools have programs in which students can earn a nursing assistant certificate or an auto mechanics certificate by the time they graduate, but students must take the right courses from the beginning to succeed in these programs. Other students may be interested in courses that prepare them for advanced placement tests for college. The counselor also discusses different types of diplomas that may be given by the school. For example, some have an attendance diploma for those who attended school but did not pass state exit exams, a diploma for those meeting all basic requirements including passing the exams, and an honors diploma for those who took and passed a rigorous academic program. Time should be allowed for questions from the audience.

Families of students who are going to high school the following year follow the schedule for family conferences with high school counselors or trained volunteers who can work on the student's courses for the next school year. If not all families can be reasonably accommodated after the general session, there should be sign-up sheets for other dates and times.

Options: If more than one middle school feeds into the same high school, families who cannot attend their home middle school session may be invited to another middle school's session.

Activity
College Preparation

Purpose: College preparation, applications, and financing are daunting topics for native English speakers let alone families of English language learners. Many families do not understand the importance of postsecondary education or the many opportunities available to their students. They also may not understand the implications of low high school grade point averages or poor course selection on their children's future.

Participants: High school students (freshmen through seniors) and their families

Preparation and Resources: Invitations should go out in appropriate home languages. Representatives of universities, colleges, and technical schools should be recruited for the session. The event requires a large room for a general session and another room with tables set up close to electrical outlets where the representatives of postsecondary institutions can sit and talk with students.

Description of Activity: A speaker should talk for about 30 minutes about the following topics:

- The need for postsecondary education for better employment possibilities in the United States
- The high school courses and grade point average needed for various postsecondary options
- The availability and advantages of taking advanced placement or dual-enrollment courses
- Recommendations for how many college applications to submit, when to submit them, and programs available to pay for college application fees
- Financial aid options, including scholarships, grants, work-study, and loans. Some warnings also should be made about amassing too much debt before college graduation.

Make sure to allow time for general questions from the audience and provide time for families to visit with university, college, and technical-school representatives at their tables. Also provide a page of tips for students considering postsecondary education written in the language spoken at home.

Options: Some institutions may allow seniors to fill in college application forms and financial aid application forms right at the event. Computers and trained personnel should be available to assist.

Activity
Job Fair

Purpose: When schools hold job fairs on campus, they show students that they understand the importance that students and their families place on finding after-school and weekend work, summer jobs, and full-time employment after graduation for those who are not continuing their education or are continuing part-time. Because of the tight economy, many family members will also be seeking employment. Decisions must be made in advance if the job fair is focused only on student employment or if it is focused on family employment. Will those attending the fair be required to show identification or an invitation? Will students need to be accompanied by a family member or adult?

Participants: High school students legally old enough to work and their families, employment experts, potential employers

Preparation and Resources: Information should be distributed in the languages of the families. Arrange tables near electrical outlets where potential employers and others can set up their displays. Also have separate rooms for group presentations in the dominant languages of the families.

Description of Activity: Have a speaker talk for about 30 minutes about ways of finding appropriate employment, résumés, interviews and other related topics. The speaker may be from a state or local workforce agency or a private employment service. While the speaker is talking in one room, employers and other job-related agencies can set up tables in a separate room. Stations can be provided where students can talk with potential employers, military recruiters, and employment services. There can be other stations where students receive help with their résumés and practice interview skills one-on-one. Provide a bulleted list of job-finding tips in the home languages of the families. Have sign-up sheets for teacher conferences available.

Options: Some schools have work-study programs in which high school students spend part of their school day working in the community. Counselors may set up a table to discuss these programs with students and families.

Activity
Gardening

Purpose: Gardening can involve families in a variety of ways. Schools have created gardens in boxes, on roofs, and on formerly weedy lots. They grow gardens for food, educaton, and birds and butterflies. These projects can be as small or large as desired. States may have agricultural extension programs or master gardener programs where people who are experts in gardening at the local level serve as resources for people interested in starting gardens.

Participants: Families, students, school personnel, and other community members

Preparation and Resources: Have land or planters ready for planting. Make sure they will receive enough natural light and that water is easily accessible. Also have dirt, seeds, and shovels or trowels.

Description of Activity: Interested families should meet and come up with a plan for the garden. Plan on whether seeds will be purchased or families will bring seeds and clippings from their own gardens. Plan planting days and include as many families as possible. Come up with a plan for weeding, watering, and caring for the garden. If herbs, vegetables, or other products will be harvested, come up with a plan for harvesting and distributing them.

Options: Schools can come up with many ways to make this activity more personal:

- Families can donate plants that represent their culture and share information about the plants with students and other families.
- Flowers can be dried, pressed, and made into artwork.
- Families can build bird houses and baths or stepping stones for larger gardens.
- Fruits and vegetables can be cooked into nutritious meals.

Activity
Presentations by Other Organizations

Purpose: Many organizations will jump at an opportunity to share information about their organization with groups of families and children. However, some presenters may not understand the need for interactive sessions that are easy to understand. If this is the case, then school personnel can limit the presentation to about 15 minutes and provide related materials that will get the families actively engaged. The sessions should be based on the interests expressed by the families. (See Chapter 2.) Special attention should be paid to the needs of families of English language learners. For example, some organizations provide free English lessons or materials in various languages.

Participants: Families with children. Representatives of community organizations.

Preparation: Contact the organization and set up a time for the presentation. Ask about people from the organization who can provide sessions in languages other than English. Ask about activities that the families can do during the presentation and about materials they can take home with them.

Description of Activity:
- Public library: Someone from the public library can come to explain the process of applying for a library card, checking out books or other materials, and other free services that the library offers, such as use of the Internet. The library representative can also discuss special programs, such as summer reading programs or storytelling for young children. Families can even fill out an application for a library card during the meeting. This can be tied to an interactive read-aloud in which families participate. An example would be Eric Carle's *From Head to Toe* in which families can move as the animals in the book move.
- Public transportation system: In larger cities, almost everyone takes advantage of the public transportation systems, but in small cities and towns, many people may not be familiar with the bus systems. Someone from the public transit system could discuss routes and times for bus service. They could also discuss the cost, where to buy tickets, and special discounts for students, senior citizens, or monthly passes. This could be accompanied by a read-aloud or sing-along of a song such as the "Wheels on the Bus."
- Fire department: The fire safety personnel are charged with presenting fire prevention programs. They are often busy during fire prevention week but would be happy to do a presentation for children and parents at another time during the year. Copy small booklets on fire prevention tips in advance and provide students with crayons, markers, and/or colored pencils to illustrate the books. Make sure the tips are available in the native languages of the families.

- ◆ Police department: The police department has various public safety presentations for audiences of different ages. After the discussion, families can get into small groups by language to discuss ways they can reduce crime and increase safety for their children. Ideas can be written on chart paper and shared with the whole group with translation as necessary. For example, families of older students may come up with safe activities that their adolescents can do in the evenings and on weekends. Families of younger students may come up with a volunteer crossing guard or playground monitor programs depending on their concerns.
- ◆ Health fair: Various community health organizations can set up booths around the school or playground to provide families with information and to do blood pressure, eyesight, hearing, or other screenings.

Options: Depending on your community, there are many community organizations that may want to provide information to families at your school. There may be museums, zoos, community theater, and nature centers to name a few. Contact the Chamber of Commerce to find out about private businesses that will be willing to come to the school. In order not to favor one business over another, send out invitations to all of that type of business in the community or neighborhood. For example, someone could do a general presentation about cell-phone safety and etiquette, and then different companies could have booths around the cafeteria or gym to demonstrate their newest technology. There could be a presentation on pet care, and then veterinarians could share information about the services they offer.

Activity
Continuing Education

Purpose: Schools can provide facilities for adult continuing education and information to families about continuing education possibilities from local colleges. The better educated the families are, the more they will understand what their children are learning at school and be able to support them. Bringing families into the school for continuing education will make them more comfortable coming to school and participating in meetings concerning their children's education.

Participants: Continuing education teachers and family members

Preparation and Resources: Contact local colleges to determine if they are interested in providing continuing education classes on your campus. Contact organizations that provide English lessons, GED classes, or technology sessions. Make sure classroom space is available after school or on weekends.

Description of Activity: Provide information to families about continuing education courses and financial aid possibilities. Make sure space is available on a regular basis for the courses scheduled; this may include having to reschedule maintanance and security crews.

Options: Family members could provide sessions for each other, including computer classes, art classes, or dance classes. Families of English language learners could teach other families their native language.

Resources

Multicultural Books

My Name Is María Isabel/Me llamo María Isabel, by Alma Flor Ada (1995), is a chapter book for young readers emphasizing the importance of names to identity, especially for English language learners. María Isabel, who was named after her grandmothers, went to school first in Puerto Rico and later at a bilingual school on the mainland, but when she came to an all-English-speaking school, her teacher called her Mary Lopez because there were already two Marías in the class. María missed out on a part in the holiday program because she didn't respond to her name as Mary Lopez. María Isabel doesn't say anything to her teacher until she has an opportunity to write an essay on her "greatest wish." After reading the essay, the teacher begins calling her by the correct name and gives her a singing part in the program.

One Green Apple, by Eve Bunting (2006), is a picture book that helps young children understand how it feels to be an immigrant and not belong. On Farah's second day at school in the United States, the class takes a field trip to an apple orchard. She notices the differences between herself and the other children, such as the dupatta that covers her head. The boys and girls all sit together on the hay wagon, something they would never do in her home country, which is not mentioned by name in the book. She picks one green apple and adds it to the red apples the other children have put in the machine to make apple cider. Although her apple is different, she believes it adds something extra to the cider. She reflects that she is different but she can still be a part of the group, just like her different apple became part of the cider. Some of the children make an extra effort to get to know her, and she says "apple," her first English word.

Return to Sender, by Julia Alvarez (2009), is a story told in alternating chapters from the viewpoints of Tyler and Mari, two fifth graders with very different backgrounds, whose lives intersect. Tyler grew up on a dairy farm in Vermont. After Tyler's grandfather dies, his father is crippled in a tractor accident, and his older brother goes to college, they are forced to hire illegal migrant workers or lose the farm. Mari is the daughter of one of the migrant workers and is in the same class at school with Tyler. This is primarily a story of growing friendships across cultures but it also illuminates the challenges faced by children of illegal immigrants in the United States, which often affects their schooling. They move for better jobs, children have many responsibilities at home, families are often separated, and children may be kept home from school when they fear deportation.

Websites

Kids Gardening

www.kidsgardening.org

> This website, sponsored by the National Gardening Association, explains the benefits of school gardens and the different types of gardens found at schools across the country. It has numerous examples of successful gardens and ways to include families and the community in the projects. In addition, the site offers grant and fundraising ideas.

Making Books

www.makingbooks.com and http://blog.susangaylord.com

> A website and blog by Susan Kapusanski Gaylord describe making books with children. The sites have myriad ideas for teachers and families. They talk about topics for books, ways to make books, and ways to make illustrations. Gaylord includes information on the use of recycled materials. She believes bookmaking helps all families understand that their culture and experiences are valuable.

Movie Nights

www.movlic.com/k12/programming.html and http://falmouth.patch.com/articles/movie-night-rocks-at-north-falmouth-elementary-school

> The first website is from Movie Licensing USA, which explains how to get a license to legally show movies at family movie nights. It also has a number of tips for successful family movie nights, including how to choose movies, how to promote movie nights, and how to incorporate a concession stand or other money-making activities. The second website is from North Falmouth Elementary School in Massachusetts and describes one of their movie nights.

National Museum of Mexican Art

www.nationalmuseumofmexicanart.org/pages/edu_part.html

> The museum's website describes ways that the museum partners with the Chicago public schools. This shows how schools and museums, nature centers, musical groups, and other community organizations can partner with schools.

Orville Wright Garden Club

http://theorvillewrightgardenclub.blogspot.com

> The Orville Wright Garden Club involves students and teachers from Orville Wright Middle School, family members, and interested community members in gardening. This blog is a continuing description in photos and words of gardening projects at the school such as growing fruit trees, creating a butterfly garden, and composting. The blog is designed to report group activities to participants but could also provide ideas for other schools interested in starting their own gardening club.

Parent Teacher Organization

www.ptotoday.com

> This website has information on how to form and run a parent teacher organization. It has many ideas on building a multicultural organization, including "Connecting with Immigrant Parents" and "Overcome the Language Barrier." The site also has a section on different types of events and programs that will attract diverse families.

Vine Hill Elementary School

www.vinehill.santacruz.k12.ca.us/PTA/familyfun.htm

> This site has information about the Family Fun Nights that Vine Hill Elementary School Parent Teacher Association in California has put on since 2004. It has a variety of ideas that could be implemented in other locations.

Other Resources

Auerbach, S. (2009). Walking the walk: Portraits in leadership for family engagement in urban schools. *The School Community Journal.* 19(1), pp. 9–32.

5

Making the Most of Family Contacts

Scenario
Report Card Conferences

Each fall, all teachers at Napa Elementary School in Northern California are required to speak with families before releasing the first six-week report card. The idea is to establish communication with the families early in the year and to make the families aware of any potential problems with their children at school. Some families come before or immediately after school while others come during the teachers' conference time. However, many families take advantage of conferences that are set up from 6 to 8:30 p.m. on the first Tuesday after report cards come out. A large number of families wanted to come during that time, so Mrs. Harris, an experienced second-grade teacher, had to set up conferences every 15 minutes.

Darshan Patel, his mother, and his younger sister, Smita, came in promptly at 7:30 for their conference. Although Darshan was listed as an English language learner who spoke Gujarati as his native language, he had developed enough English to function well in Mrs. Harris's all-English classroom. It never occurred to Mrs. Harris to ask for a translator for this conference. Darshan and Mrs. Patel sat down in chairs set up for the conference, and Smita sat in Mrs. Patel's lap. Because of her rushed schedule, Mrs. Harris thanked them for coming and immediately took out Darshan's report card to review. Mrs. Harris explained that Darshan was doing well in all subjects and behaved well. The teacher asked Mrs. Patel if she had any questions about the report card and she said, "no." Then the teacher explained that she was concerned that Darshan rarely participated in class discussions and did not talk very much when working in cooperative groups. Mrs. Patel did not respond to Mrs. Harris's comments but asked in halting English if Darshan did all his work, and Mrs. Harris answered that he did, much to the obvious pleasure of his mother. Mrs. Harris asked if there was anything else Mrs. Patel wanted to know. When Mrs. Patel said "no," Mrs. Harris walked them to the door and called in the next family.

When Mrs. Patel went home, she told her husband in Gujarati about the meeting with the teacher. He asked if she had mentioned that other children were picking on Darshan at school, and Mrs. Patel said that the teacher had not brought up this topic so she felt it would be rude to question the teacher about this problem. She shared her pride in Darshan's discipline and hard work at school with her husband. She also reported the teacher's strange comments about Darshan not talking enough at school.

In reflecting on the conferences, Mrs. Harris felt they had gone well even though she had not had as much time as she wished with each family. She had given everyone an opportunity to ask questions and expressed her concerns about the children's progress.

Cultural Differences

As the scenario indicates, culture as well as language may be a barrier to effective communication. Families of English language learners often have different experiences and cultural expectations of school. Hanson and Lynch (2004) have identified different factors that may create difficulties in cross-cultural communication and expectations. Cultures vary in the space between people during a conversation, ways of holding a conversation, and how time is treated. Some cultures place more emphasis on individuality, while others place more on teamwork. In some cultures, age and wisdom is highly esteemed while other cultures focus more on youth and the future. All of these factors may impact the communication between schools and families. For example, a teacher may have a conference with a family member. The teacher may come from a culture in which people take turns speaking and allow the other person to complete their thought before interjecting an idea. The family member may come from a culture in which several people speak at once. The teacher may find the family member rude because he keeps interrupting, and the family member may believe the teacher is not interested in his ideas. Sometimes there are also differring views of time. A teacher may schedule several conferences one right after another. A family member, who believes that one spends as much time on a task as necessary to complete it, may find it disconcerting when the conference is ended before all pertinent issues have been discussed.

Underlying Assumptions

American schools can be very uncomfortable places for families of English language learners. The language and culture of the school may be quite different from the families' previous schooling experiences. Schools cannot assume that families of ELLs will be able to easily gain familiarity with and access to school policies and procedures. They cannot think that translating school documents into a home language such as Spanish or Vietnamese is sufficient. Schools must recognize that they make many assumptions that families of ELLs know how American schools work. For example, grading systems are different in other countries and families may not even realize the significance of an A or a D, an S or a U. Navigating schools when one has a different language and culture makes school engagement difficult unless schools make an effort to reach out to families of ELLs and provide them with the needed knowledge and tools. Schools cannot jump to the conclusion that families of ELLs are disinterested or are less capable of being involved in their child's education. Rather, schools must focus strategically on building the capacity of all families to become effectively involved in schools.

The following is a real example with names changed of a school that made mistaken assumptions about families of ELLs and their interest level in their child's schooling. Sample Elementary School was nearing the end of the first six weeks of grading. Its teachers were dismayed that some students had failing grades and that these students' parents had made no contact with the school. Teacher discussions centered on particular disappointment with the families of English language learners that were not checking student grades online to monitor progress. Grades were posted faithfully by the teachers, and all parents had immediate and ongoing access to their children's grades.

Teachers noted that Sample Elementary School's handbook was online and contained a special section for parents about online grading. The grading section provided detailed instructions on how to open a parent account to access grades, including an invitation to visit the school office to open an account. The school was especially proud that its website and office staff were bilingual. Sample Elementary School considered its bilingual website and the purchase of an online grading system valuable tools that would lead to increased involvement of all families. Teachers were puzzled about why parents did not care about their child's progress and would not make time to check on grades.

Families, on the other hand, liked the fact that students brought home graded papers on a daily basis. They were able to see the grades their children were earning and could review the work. Several families even made it a point to get together to discuss and compare their children's work. They had no idea that Sample Elementary teachers were disappointed and regarded them as uninterested in their children's schooling.

Sample Elementary School failed to take into account the background knowledge and support needed by the ELL families to navigate the school system, in particular online grading. The school faculty made the assumption that all families knew the school maintained a website that contained important school information. The school assumed parents knew to look online for the handbook that had the online grading information. The school also assumed families were comfortable communicating online and understood that the campus was governed by certain grading policies. Parents were expected to take time off from work to come to the school at the time when the school office was open. No consideration was given to parent work hours, available transportation, or child-care needs. Additionally, the school assumed parents would have readily available Internet access.

Sample Elementary School assumed they had effective family communication tools in place. However, the school did not stop to consider the specific background knowledge needed in order for all families, especially families of English language learners, to make use of the school website and online grading. It was easy to jump to the conclusion that certain families did not care about student achievement.

Differing expectations were also evident in the authors' local community during Charro Days, which celebrates the friendship between Matamoros, Mexico, and Brownsville, Texas. As part of the weeklong celebration, students participate in numerous performances such as school dance programs, festivals, and parades. Many students dress in traditional costumes from the various states of Mexico. Private and public schools give students the afternoon off from school to participate in a children's parade. A vacation day follows the parade day.

Some parents new to the area thought that participation was voluntary, especially considering that the appropriate costumes could be expensive, and decided to keep their child home the day of the parade. Parents were shocked to find that their child would receive an F in social studies if he or she didn't have a costume and participate in the festivities. The school and the parents did not have a shared understanding of the importance of the event.

Schools should take the time to determine to what extent its communication is effective with the families of English language learners. Communication methods should be regularly reviewed to determine if the school is operating with underlying assumptions about families' familiarity with school culture and knowledge of school operations. The following are some questions that might be asked:

- ◆ How does the school communicate with families?
- ◆ Are all families receiving the messages in language they can understand?
- ◆ What background knowledge is needed to understand messages posted online or sent home?
- ◆ Could there be differing expectations due to the way schools are operated in different parts of the world or even within the United States?

Scenario
Lack of Engagement

Riverside Elementary School decided to find out why families of English language learners were not attending many events at school. Riverside Elementary is situated in a middle-class neighborhood of single-family homes that were built around the school in the 1960s as the suburban area gained population. The school had always prided itself on its high level of family involvement in school activities. Family volunteers were common, and the PTA was active. As the neighborhood aged, fewer and fewer children were zoned to the school from the local neighborhood, and in order to keep the school open, the zoning area of the school was increased to include a large apartment complex on the other side of a busy roadway. The school district arranged for buses to carry the children to and from school each day. The children who were from the apartment complex were from working-class families, and the majority of them spoke English as a second language.

The teachers at Riverside were highly expectant as they waited for the school year to begin. They had glowing reports from the schools where the children had previously been zoned about how hardworking the children were and how respectful the families were. They were baffled, however, when the school's kindergarten roundup, one of the signature family encounters, was attended by only a handful of children who were mostly from the local neighborhood. An open house also failed to draw many families, and teachers really became upset when a day set up for family conferences became chaotic when families were late for appointments, which complicated the schedules of the handful of interpreters that the school had available. Some families also brought younger siblings, which teachers felt distracted from the important conference time. The teachers were especially disappointed because they wanted to discuss why many of the children were silent in class, refusing to answer even when they seemed to know the answer.

After getting an earful about what a disaster the conferences were and complaining about the indifference of the families to their children's education, the principal decided to find out what was going on. A small team of school personnel and an interpreter went to the apartment complex in search of an explanation. After talking with several families, they went back to the school with their findings. Primarily, they found that most of the families relied on public transportation. The public transportation was good at getting them to work but did not come anywhere near the suburban school. To get to the school, they had to rely on neighbors who had cars. Use of the car was usually on the neighbor's schedule rather than the carefully orchestrated schedule of the school. Many said they were willing to walk to the school, but the busy roadway between the apartment complex and the school kept them at home, especially since many of them would have to bring all of their children because they did not have child care. The team also found that in the grounds of the apartment complex, the children seemed to be happy as they played together. The silent children from the classroom were active, loud, and talkative. The team learned that at the new school many of the children had been teased during recess because of their Spanish accents and that they remained silent to avoid being ridiculed.

After finding out more about the families and their environment, the school set out to regain its position as one of the leading schools for family involvement. Bronfenbrenners Ecological Systems Theory (Brofenbrenner, 1979) can help schools understand situations like this. The theory emphasizes that to fully understand the students, schools must understand their environment at home and at school. In addition, they must understand the relationship between the school and families. In this case, the children behaved differently at home, which they perceived as a safe environment, than at school, where they were afraid of being teased. The school-family relationship was also impacted by transportation. The children got to school every day, but they came on school buses. The teachers in their cars never noticed what a barrier the busy roadway might be for the family members without cars. Without knowing the entire context, it is difficult to know exactly why certain behaviors are occuring, something Riverside was able to resolve after gaining new information. The point of this discussion on Riverside Elementary is that communication can be very complicated and influenced by many factors. We often hear when a new program is introduced that veteran teachers will say, "I'll just shut my door and hope they leave me alone." When developing relationships with families, it is important not to have our doors closed, but rather to be open to the many ways that people communicate.

Relationship Building

In Chapter 1, we mentioned awareness, respect, and communication as being the foundation for building relationships with families of English language learners, and we return to these concepts here. As the examples earlier in this chapter illustrate, educators need to learn as much as possible about the families of English language learners and try to understand the world from their perspective. When people behave differently than we expect, it is easy to place blame before discovering the underlying causes. As communication grows, so too will trust and respect on both sides.

Working with both preservice and practicing teachers, we have often heard about bad experiences with families of school-aged children, but when these teachers worked with families one-on-one, their attitudes shifted dramatically. In one program, we introduced future teachers to children and families through an after-school tutoring program. We had our students work with an individual child on developing literacy skills. The students also had to have two-way communication with the family members who brought the child to the program through informal discussions and formal conferencing. While reflecting with our future teacher candidates, we were amazed at how much they were learning through this communication with families. Although all of our students were preparing to teach in either bilingual or ESL settings, they often felt their communication skills with the families were complicated. Explaining academic terminology to family members who were not up on the latest academic jargon was difficult. And it was difficult for bilingual students to find an adequate translation for words learned only in English. Our students also realized that their teacher preparation program had not prepared them to work with families. They had been placed in classrooms for observations, but few had previous opportunities to actually communicate one-on-one with a family member. Finally, because our students had to work so closely with family members, they began to feel a great deal more empathy and respect for them. One day, the roads flooded and many of the tutors and professors had a hard time reaching the school and wondered if any of the families would show up. But the families rolled up their pants and walked through the water to make sure their children got to the tutoring session. Seen from a distance, the families often seemed intimidating or detached. When met face to face with the child's best interest at heart, they found that families were deeply involved and committed to their children's success in school.

Communication

When families and schools interact in two-way communication, they will grow to understand one another, but communicating with families of English language learners can be challenging in many ways. Educators face the same challenges that they do with all families. When and how should you communicate with the family? Should it be in person before or after school or by appointment, by telephone during the day or evening, by e-mail, text, or notes? How can communication be truly two-way? In addition to these common issues, educators also face language and cultural challenges with families of English language learners.

Translation

Teachers sometimes assume that the family members of a student who speaks English fluently will also speak English well. However, family members may not have had the same educational opportunities in English as the student and may not speak English fluently. Before conferences, phone calls, or letters home, the teachers should find out what language or languages are spoken at home by family members responsible for the student's progress at school and determine whether they have a common language with the family. Although brief encounters with family members before and after school can be translated by the child, formal conferences, telephone conversations, or letters should be translated by someone who knows English, knows the family's language, and has an understanding of school policies and procedures. Although many children speak English more fluently than their adult family members, using them or other family members as translators should be avoided for a number of reasons. First, the process of translating important information from the school to the family may change family dynamics. Second, the family member may not have the vocabulary to translate complex educational issues. And third, the family member may be reluctant to convey negative information.

The authors have learned through their own mistakes that a good translator is much more than someone who speaks the family's language. Many languages have different dialects and use different words depending on the region of origin. Although people may speak a language well enough for daily interactions, they may lack the technical language in English or the other language to translate educational issues. People who speak a language fluently don't always write fluently and care must be taken that letters that go home are professionally done, as families may wonder about the school's competency if a letter is filled with grammatical or spelling errors in their native language. Lynch and Hanson (2004) say that effective translators are proficient in the dialect of the family, understand cross-cultural communication, and understand the content that needs to be conveyed to the families. They also provide guidelines for working with translators. The first step is working with the translator in advance of an important meeting to explain the ideas that they wish to convey to the family and any documents that will be presented to the family in English. Many words do not translate directly from English to another language so it is important that the translator understands the concepts in advance rather than trying to translate word for word or sentence by sentence as the meeting progresses. During meetings, educators should look at the family rather than the translator and stop frequently to allow ideas to be translated and for families to ask questions. Also, educators should try to learn a couple of phrases, such as "welcome" and "thank you" in the family's native language and make sure that they do not use any body language or gestures that might be offensive. Translators also must keep information discussed during the meetings confidential.

There are many different ways to communicate with families. A variety of methods should be used in order to reach as many families of English language learners as possible. The following is a partial list of various means of communication and some special considerations for families of English language learners.

Notes and Newsletters

Notes and newletters should be in the home language. If staff are not available to translate notes into the home language, try to find a family member of your students who can translate notes that are going out to all families. Notes that go out about the progress of an individual student need to be kept confidential and should be translated by a professional. When inviting families to events at school, students can assist with writing or illustrating the note. For example, a note can be copied onto one half of a piece of paper and students can illustrate the other half. A note written or illustrated by a child is much more likely to be noticed than one copied on a machine. The child can address the note to the appropriate person or people who are likely to come to the event. If the teacher is addressing the notes individually, he should put "To the family of _____ (child's name)" unless he is sure of family members' names. Simply addressing it "To Mr. and Mrs. _____ (child's last name)" is likely to be wrong and alienate some families.

Anthony Elementary School in south central Kansas has a newsletter written by parents for parents whose children are new to kindergarten. The intent of the newsletter is to help familiarize new families with school routines, procedures, schedules, and special events. The newsletter presents the parent/family perspective of what information is important for new families to know about the school. Anthony Elementary School's unique newsletter could be adapted as an outreach tool for use with families of English language learners. (See websites.) Schools would first identify the various ethnic subgroups that exist in their school community. Once such groups are identified, the school would develop and produce a newsletter for these families in their native language. This newsletter would be based on what families of a particular cultural background identify as important information for the new families to know. Schools may have families that are willing to take on the project or community members that would be excited to complete such a project. School staff may find that they need to take the lead by interviewing culturally and linguistically diverse families in order to gather the information for the family newsletter. Outside translation support may be needed if school staff does not have the ability to translate the newsletter into the needed languages. Schools may also find it helpful to work with community representatives in the development and production of the newsletter. Such representatives may be able to help gather information for the newsletters and offer valuable insight as to issues they may have seen and heard discussed by families in the community. It is also important that community representatives preview the newsletter before it goes out to ensure that it is culturally appropriate and that the right meanings are conveyed.

The family newsletters can be displayed in a designated parent space at the school and be given out in welcome packets when new families join the school. Businesses and churches may also be willing to pass on the newsletters to new families. The family newsletter can also serve as an education tool for the school's entire staff. It will help to build awareness of what culturally and linguistically diverse families regard as important school information. Faculties and staff can also choose to regularly review the new family newsletter and can embed such discussions into faculty meetings or faculty in-service days. Such information is especially important for those teachers new to the community to help them welcome parents in an effective way.

Additional family school newsletters could be produced at various times throughout the school year in order to help all families stay connected to the school. Families should be encouraged to suggest topics for special editions. However, it is important that schools first begin by focusing on an initial welcoming newsletter. The family newsletter will need to be updated on an annual basis. School information may change and families may offer feedback on the content that needs to be included.

School Phone

The school should have a plan for what to do when someone calls who does not speak the language of the person answering the phone for the school. It may be best to have some standard phrases in several different languages with pronunciation guides, so the person answering the phone can determine the language of the person calling, determine if the person calling has an emergency, and if not take a number so someone who speaks the family's native language can call back later. Another alternative is to have a prerecorded message in several languages that asks the families to leave a message on an answering machine so someone can call them later with information in their native language.

If an educator does not speak the same language as the family but wishes to speak to them on the phone, the educator should find someone to translate in advance using the guidelines discussed under the translation section of this chapter. Even if the translator knows what to communicate to the family, it is important that the educator is present when the phone call is made so he can answer any questions that the family may have rather than placing the translator in the uncomfortable position of trying to answer policy or education questions.

Conferences

Try to spread out conference times and dates so that most families will have an opportunity to attend and each conference will not be as rushed. Don't try to discuss individual student issues when members of other families are present, such as during open houses. After most of the individual conferences have been completed, make an extra effort to contact families who have not come. Perhaps they are unable to come to the school but would be willing to meet you at the neighborhood community center or someplace else closer to their home. Even just one face-to-face meeting can make an enormous difference because families will be more willing to work with teachers on solving problems that arise later, even if later contact is just by phone or letter. (See websites for tips.)

With families of English language learners, it is important to know whether the person coming for the conference will speak English or another language that you speak. If there is not a common language, then it is important to find a translator in advance rather than depending on your student or an older sibling to do the translation during the conference. Conferences are a good time to give families important information about their child's progress, but they are also a good time for teachers to learn more about the child from the family perspective. The following are some questions that could be asked of families of English language learners.

♦ Who is responsible for getting the child ready and dropping the child off every day?
♦ Who picks the child up and cares for the child after school?
♦ How much time do they spend in child care?
♦ What languages are used in the home and by whom? (grandparents, parents, television, siblings)
♦ What are the child's experiences traveling between the two cultures? Have they ever left the United States or do they travel back and forth on a regular basis?

Prepare brief notes in advance for each child so that you will remember all the important points to make and can take notes during the conference. As with all families, begin with something positive about the child. Use this time to gain information from the families about the child's favorite activites at home. This can be especially valuable information when choosing books to read or topics to write about later. Ask what the student enjoys about school and if the student has mentioned any concerns about school to the family. If possible, share the student's work samples with the family so they can see what the student is doing in class. If there are any concerns about the work, it is easier to show the family rather than just tell them about it. When it is necessary to use educational jargon, make sure to explain the terminology. For example, "your child had some trouble with the *fluency* portion of the test that measures how quickly a student reads and how many errors he makes." End with an upbeat message and try to give the family something to take home. There are some websites online that provide handouts in a variety of languages. For example, The Colorín Colorado website is a free multilingual site for families and educators of English language learners. Reading tip sheets for parents of kindergarten through grade three are available in eleven languages: Arabic, Chinese, Haitian Creole, Hmong, Korean, Navajo, Russian, Spanish, Tagalog and Vietnamese. (See websites.)

Teacher Home Visit Program

Sacramento City Unified School District in California has found that home visits are one of the most effective ways of reaching culturally and linguistically diverse families. A dedicated link can be found on the district's website about the Parent Teacher Home Visit Project (PTHVP). (See websites.) The project describes itself as

> an inexpensive and easily replicated model of family engagement that has been proven to end the cycle of blame between families and school staff by building trust and respect, instilling cultural competency and increasing personal and professional capacity for all involved.

The model behind the PTHVP involves a cycle of two rounds of home visits, one in the fall and another in the spring of the school year. The sequence of events begins with training staff for a first home visit in the fall. Training topics include listening and building relationships. The first visit also includes a personal invitation to the school's first parent teacher night. Following the first visit, staff members are debriefed and receive additional training on conducting home visits that focus on academics. The second teacher home visit occurs in the spring with its focus on how families can support children's school success. The cycle is then evaluated and planning implemented for the following fall.

Many districts and campuses across the United States utilize the PTHVP model. One such school is Fairview Elementary School in Denver, Colorado. More than 275 home visits were made to 145 households in one school year. The project supports the goal of increasing family engagement, is included as part of Fairview's school improvement plan, and is supported by a grant from the National Education Association.

Community Outreach

Some families prefer not to have visitors in their home, and some teachers may feel uncomfortable going to homes, especially alone. Therefore, some school districts have replaced home visits, which are more personal, with visits to community centers, local churches, or other locations where many people from the community gather. This is especially important for families of English language learners, who may not feel comfortable at school or may not have transportation to get to school. Clergymen can serve as liasons between the school and parishoners who have children at the school.

Families to Families

Most families gain a great deal of information about school from other families. This is especially true of families of English language learners, who are much more likely to contact someone who speaks their language than call the school and struggle to communicate. Unfortunately, this information is not always accurate. The school can still take advantage of this method of communication by enlisting family members from various language and cultural backgrounds and providing them with accurate information. Recruit volunteers who have had children at your school for at least a year and are willing to help contact other families. Try to get as many volunteers who speak a language other than English as possible. Then provide these volunteers with important information that the school would like to be communicated to families, such as school hours, grading systems, required immunizations, upcoming meetings, and homework policies. Provide them with the information in writing in the languages that they will be using and make sure that both the volunteers and the families they contact have names, telephone numbers, and e-mails of people who can provide answers to their questions. Then ask the volunteers to contact other families in their neighborhood. If they are not comfortable going door to door, they can contact people at other local meeting places, including grocery stores, churches, and parks. One of the authors remembers getting some of the best information about her children's elementary school from other families whose children were playing at the local park.

Designated Parent Space

For many schools, a family/parent resource center is not possible because space is limited. One alternative to a formal resource center is to identify a specific space as an information area for parents. School information on a variety of topics in multiple languages may be displayed there. Such information may include school calendars, newsletters, and upcoming events including family workshops and meetings. Brochures on a wide variety of topics related to nutrition, health, how to support student success in school, and so on may also be displayed. This designated family area is useful for displaying community resources. A list of helpful phone numbers may also be displayed.

An attractive bulletin board display will enhance such an area with phrases such as "welcome families" in a variety of languages that reflect the languages spoken throughout the school community. Photos depicting family involvement in the school may also be displayed. Additionally, the space may include photos of key school personnel such as the principal, counselor, family liaison, etc. This allows families to put names and faces together for key personnel in the school.

A faculty or staff member should be assigned to update the family information space on a regular basis. Schools fortunate enough to have a family liaison may add the upkeep of this information area to the liaison's list of responsibilities. All school staff should be encouraged to contribute ideas for the space. Additionally, ideas should be solicited from families as to what information they would like to see available in the space.

Families will learn to seek out this area to learn more about the school. Signs clearly identifying the location of this family information area should be highly visible so that all visitors will see it when they enter the school. Ideally, the space should be located near the main school entrance or perhaps within the school's main office.

Families of ELLs will appreciate finding information about how the U.S. school system works. Such information could include school hours, school rules, school holidays, curriculum standards, assessment information, and teacher and school expectations. Activities like pick up and drop off, school breaks, lunch breaks, and teacher communication vary greatly from country to country. Understanding how the local school handles these policies is important for families from different cultures. Culturally and linguistically diverse families will appreciate cultural explanations of American holidays such as Independence Day, Thanksgiving, and Halloween. Such explanations will help families feel more comfortable with American traditions that may be celebrated in the school.

Open Communication

It is important that both families and educators can communicate informally as well as formally. Although certain precautions need to be taken for safety and to avoid interruptions to classes, too many restrictions are likely to limit communication. It is often the quick chat before or after school that engages teachers and families in important communication. For example, teachers at a New York City elementary school needed permission from a supervisor to contact families. (See websites.) All contact had to be from school phones or e-mails during school hours. Teachers were not allowed to use personal cell phones to call families in the evening. Since communication with families is difficult to begin with, schools and districts should avoid adding extra unnecessary roadblocks.

Activity
Identifying Underlying Assumptions

Purpose: This activity is designed to help faculty and administrators carefully examine written communication that is sent home to families. It asks faculty and administrators to think about what background knowledge is necessary to understand the communication and what resources may be necessary to carry out any instructions that are included in the communication.

Participants: School faculty and administrators

Preparation and Resources: Send out an announcement for a faculty meeting. Prepare a handout or projection of the Sample Elementary School example from the beginning of the chapter. Bring copies of a recent school correspondence from your school. Also bring chart paper and markers.

Description of Activity: Review the Sample Elementary School example. Identify a piece of school correspondence that has been sent to school families on a previous occasion. This may be schoolwide correspondence or correspondence sent by a particular grade level. Ask the group what background knowledge and cultural knowledge a family would need to know to make sense of this letter. If the letter asks the families to do something, what knowledge or resources are necessary to follow through on the letter?

Options: Extend the discussion by selecting various cultural and linguistic groups within the school community and asking how the letter could be modified and adapted to ensure that parents have a full understanding of what it is they are expected to do. This discussion group may be led by a teacher leader, parent involvement representative or school administrator. Parents and community members would offer input as to what background information and cultural knowledge was needed to make sense of the selected letter. Parent and community perceptions should be compared to the school faculty's perceptions. How similar or different were the responses? What changes are needed by the school to better communicate with families of English language learners?

Do a similar activity with a grade level or subject area. Sample correspondence may include notes on parent teacher conferences; field trips; parent teacher organizations; fundraising; science fairs, etc.

Activity
Family Prompts

Purpose: This activity is designed to help educators and other staff members obtain information from families on an informal basis. This shows families that you value their knowledge about the student and their ideas.

Preparation: Create a list of open-ended questions that would be appropriate to ask families. These should be translated for teachers and staff members who are multilingual.

Description of Activity: Teachers brainstorm information that they would like from family members. For example, a teacher might want to know what a child does after school and on weekends or what the child likes best about school. Conduct a meeting with all staff members who regularly meet with families, including administrators, secretaries, and teaching assistants. Let families know that the school has started a program to get to know the students better by asking a "question of the month" to families. People who talk to a particular family during the month on the phone or in person that month can ask the question and jot down the answer to provide a more complete picture of the student.

Caution: Most questions will be viewed by family members as genuine interest in their child and respect for their knowledge about the child. Caution should be taken to avoid asking questions that might embarrass some family members or cause concern. For example, one of the authors thought the parents of a child were divorced and asked where the father lived, only to find out the answer was "prison."

Activity
What Would You Do?

Purpose: Most of the time educators have to respond to difficult communication on the spot, but this activity allows educators to think more deeply about how they would respond to difficult situations and reflect with other educators about different ways to handle these challenging conversations.

Participants: Teachers and administrators

Preparation: Prepare copies of the different scenarios for the group to discuss.

Description of Activity: Teachers and administrators will discuss the following scenarios and questions in small groups. After they discuss how each situation could be handled better, they can discuss the possible solutions with the whole group. These are real scenarios and there is no one correct answer or simple solution.

- ◆ **Scenario One.** Ms. Tan has sent three notes home with Raul, an English language learner, asking that his mother call or come to school to discuss his academic progress. After three weeks, she has received no response by phone, in writing, or in person.
  1. What could be the reasons for a lack of response?
  2. What should Ms. Tan do now in order to speak to one of Raul's family members?
- ◆ **Scenario Two.** Mr. Lopez has a conference with Mr. Sanchez, the father of Sergio, who has been involved in several fights at school with Ramiro. When Mr. Lopez asks for Mr. Sanchez's help to stop the fighting, Mr. Sanchez claims that Ramiro has been bullying Sergio and he told Sergio to stand up for himself and fight back. Mr. Sanchez asks Mr. Lopez, "Do you just want him to stand there and get beat up? I have complained about Ramiro picking on Sergio on the bus and nothing has been done."
  1. What should Mr. Lopez say to Mr. Sanchez now?
  2. What can Mr. Lopez and others do to stop the fighting?
  3. What types of policies and procedures might prevent similar problems with other students in the future?
- ◆ **Scenario Three.** Ms. Walton speaks to the mother of Meira, who is from Bosnia. Meira has been daydreaming and not completing her work at school. Through a translator, Ms. Walton asks the mother to talk to Meira about the problem. The next day, Ms. Walton asks Meira if her parents talked to her, and Meira says, "No, they just spanked me for not getting my schoolwork done."

        1. What should Ms. Walton say to Meira?

        2. What might be a more effective way to deal with children who are not completing their schoolwork?

◆ **Scenario Four.** Victor has been talking back to the teacher and being disrespectful. Ms. Garcia decides to call in his mother, who is a young single mother from the Dominican Republic. They both speak Spanish although with slightly different accents and vocabulary, since Ms. Garcia's Spanish was learned along the Texas-Mexico border rather than in the Dominican Republic like Victor's mother, Ms. Villarreal. When Ms. Garcia explains the problem at school, Ms. Villarreal says she has the same problems at home and doesn't know what to do about it. She says, "He just doesn't want to listen to me. Can you help me?"

        1. What suggestions should Ms. Garcia make to Ms. Villarreal?

        2. What resources are available at your school or in your community that might help family members who are having trouble disciplining their children?

◆ **Scenario Five.** Linda doesn't hand in her homework. After numerous tries, Linda's teacher, Ms. Maupin, reaches Linda's father by phone. Although his English is not fluent, they are able to communicate. Her father says that he works at night and that Linda and five of her cousins stay with her grandmother. The grandmother is busy taking care of babies, making meals, cleaning up, and getting children to bed. She doesn't have time to supervise Linda's homework and Linda does not have a quiet place to get it done.

        1. What should Ms. Maupin say to Linda's father?

        2. Do the homework policies at your school take into account families like Linda's?

Resources

Multicultural Books

Kids Around the World Celebrate! The Best Feasts and Festivals from Many Lands, by Lynda Jones (2000), shares festivals from all over the world that children celebrate with their families and friends. It is a collection of cultural celebrations that include background information as well as "how-to" recipes and activities.

Kids Around the World Create! The Best Crafts and Activities from Many Lands, by Arlette N. Braman (1999), is a collection of 24 crafts and activites from around the world. Each activity includes a culture link that explains how the craft is used within its culture. It helps children explore and discover customs and cultures from around the world.

Kids Around the World Play! The Best Fun and Games from Many Lands, by Arlette N. Braman (2002), is designed to help students learn about cultures from around the world through games and toys. Facts about the history and culture of each country are included.

Websites
Home Visit Project
www.pthvp.org
> This website provides information about home visit projects across the country. It also has information about training sessions and even an online video about the program.

Obstacles to Communication
www.nypost.com/p/news/local/manhattan/these_teachers_need_call_pass
_3zcKBnmGlatGKymPrF8p1I?CMP=OTC-rss&FEEDNAME=
> This article from the *New York Post* is about a New York elementary school where teachers needed a supervisor's permission to contact families. Although this may be an extreme example, many schools unintentionally put up roadblocks to parent-teacher communication.

Parent Teacher Conferences
http://nysut.org/newmember/survival_conferences.html
> This is a free website by New York United Teachers, providing tips on conducting conferences with families. It has a list of dos and don'ts for conferences.

Reading Tips in 11 Languages
www.colorincolorado.org/guides/readingtips
> Reading tips that can be downloaded and copied are provided in 11 languages on this site. Colorín Colorado's homepage at www.colorincolorado.org has resources for families, teachers, administrators, and librarians. Readers can view the site in either English or Spanish. There is an extensive list of book titles with annotations so if a family wants to find a children's book about a specific topic, they can search for the information there.

Successful Parent Involvement Practices in Kansas Schools
www.kpirc.org/resources/about/
successful-parent-involvement-practics-in-kansas-schools
> This online publication has descriptions of a variety of practical projects that will encourage family engagement, including the newsletter written by families for other families at Anthony Elementary School.

Other Resources

Brofenbrenner, U. (1979). Contexts of child rearing: Problems and prospects. *American Psychologist*, 34(10), pp. 844–850.

Hanson, M. J. & Lynch, E. W. (2004). *Understanding families: Approaches to diversity, disability, and risk*. Baltimore, MD: Paul H. Brookes.

Lynch, E. W. & Hanson, M. J. (2004). *Developing cross-cultural competence: A guide for working with children and their families* (3rd ed.). Baltimore: Paul H. Brookes.

6

Keeping the Momentum Going at Home

Scenario
Challenges Faced at Home

Mrs. Tucker had twins, Larissa and Marissa, in her fourth-grade class. Every day, the twins arrived at school on the bus, neatly dressed and groomed. Although they spoke Spanish as their first language in kindergarten, they had learned to speak, read, and write well in English by fourth grade. In fact, they came in after lunch one day a week to help with the school newspaper. They did well academically and always had their homework done before school—that is until early November. Suddenly, both girls stopped doing their homework even though they were still coming to school daily and doing well during school. Mrs. Tucker asked them if anything was wrong, but the girls just said they didn't have time to do their homework. Concerned after a couple of weeks of missing homework, Mrs. Tucker decided to make a home visit. As she pulled up to the mobile home far north of town and a long bus drive from school, she immediately knew what the problem was. They didn't have electricity. They had propane for heat, cooking, and hot water, but they lacked electricity for lights. The girls had done their homework regularly until early November because that was when daylight savings ended, and it was now dark by the time they arrived home.

Although this real scenario is extreme, it does point out that teachers often do not understand the adversities that children and their families face at home. It also shows the tremendous effort that some families must make to keep their children healthy, clean, fed, clothed, and at school each day. Not all families have the same resources available for homework or participating in the education of their children, yet they still want the best education possible for their children.

Homework is one of the first things that educators think about when school-home connections are discussed. Proponents of homework argue that it provides extra practice on strategies taught at school, that it improves the connection between school and home, and that it teaches students responsibility. However, recent studies are questioning all of those assumptions.

Homework

There is no evidence that more homework or any homework in elementary school or middle school improves achievement, and there is just a small improvement in achievement in high school (Kohn, 2007). Despite the fact that homework provides the least academic benefit for young children, it increased from an average of 44 minutes a week to 120 minutes per week for children six to eight years old from 1983 to 2003 (Dudley-Marling, 2003). An international study conducted in 50 nations did not find any relationship between the amount of homework assigned and the academic achievement of students. Some nations, such as Japan and Denmark, which scored highest on international measures of math and science achievement, gave little homework. Other nations, such as Thailand, Greece, and Iran, gave heavy homework but scored low in academic achievement in math and science (physorg.com, 2005).

Although it is generally assumed that homework teaches responsibility, there is no research that supports that conclusion. There are often factors beyond students' control that impact their ability to do homework. Extended families may live in a small apartment or home in order to share resources, but there may not be a quiet place to complete homework. Other students may have chores, child-care responsibilities, or religious or other after-school activities that do not allow them to complete their work at home. Most studies of homework have been conducted with middle-class English-speaking families (Dudley-Marling, 2003). Even if time and quiet space are available, students who come from families where no one else speaks English may not have anyone who can support them when they struggle with homework assignments.

Not only are the benefits of homework much less than generally assumed, but there are negative effects of homework, especially too much homework. Homework takes time away from other activities and erodes family relations.

Family members want to make sure they meet the expectations of the school by having their children do homework, but it often ends up in battles over completing homework before doing other activities, even eating dinner (Dudley-Marling, 2003). Instead of improving school-home connections, homework often creates resentment toward teachers and schools (Kohn, 2007).

The National Parent Teacher Association and the National Education Association recommend no more than 10 minutes of homework per night for each grade level so a first grader should have no more than 10 minutes, a fifth grader no more than 50 minutes, and a high school senior no more than two hours. (See websites.) The quality as well as the quantity of the homework should be considered. Rather than requiring a specific amount of homework each day, teachers should assign homework when it will extend classroom learning without causing undo stress on students or families. Just as schoolwork is adapted for the different needs of students, homework should also be adapted (Vatterott, na). Teachers should consider that students who struggle to complete their work at school will probably struggle even more at home where the teacher is not available to provide assistance.

In addition, educators should avoid assignments that require resources, such as computers, Internet access, poster board, or markers. Although cooperative learning may work well at school, group assignments outside of school should be avoided because students may not be able to get together outside of school or even call each other. Some school districts have reduced the consequences of not completing homework. In one Vermont district, homework is now worth only 10 percent of students' grades rather than 40 percent, and students are no longer kept in from recess for incomplete homework. When a large percentage of a grade is based on homework, students may understand concepts but receive low grades simply because they do not finish their homework.

Based on the information available about homework, educators should ask themselves some questions about homework policies:

- ◆ What is the purpose of homework?
- ◆ Does the amount and type of homework being given support that purpose?
- ◆ How is homework affecting students' grades and opportunities at school?
- ◆ Is homework adapted for ELLs or struggling students?
- ◆ Is homework appropriate for students who lack resources at home?
- ◆ Is homework likely to create resentment or closer relations within families?

Beyond Homework

When considering how to keep the momentum going at home, educators should think beyond homework assignments. Families support children's education by explaining to them the importance of school. Many families of ELLs are immigrants who did not have educational opportunities themselves, but they still stress the importance of school to their children based on their own life stories (Delgado-Gaitan, 2004). In fact, some of them immigrated to the United States, in part, to provide a better education for their children. Schools should value this contribution to students' education and thank families for their continued support.

A study by the Program for International Student Assessment (PISA in Focus, 2011) of 15-year-old students around the world found that students of parents who spoke to them regularly about school, books, social issues, and even television shows scored significantly higher on reading assessments than students of parents who didn't. The difference between scores remained regardless of socioeconomic levels. Some families don't feel they can help 15-year-olds with their high school homework, but they can still talk to them and this makes a difference.

Many families of ELLs don't think they can help with their child's education because they do not speak English or they lack literacy in their home language. Therefore, it is important to let families know that what they already do at home is helping their child's education, and they can help their child more even if they don't speak English, don't read or write, or have little extra time. Many of the activities recommended in this chapter are oral and can be conducted in the native language.

One way that families of ELLs can help their children in school is by speaking to them more in their native language. Research indicates that families who report "sometimes" having dinnertime discussions about school, course or program selection, or interesting school-related activities significantly increase the academic achievement of their children even if they do not participate in school-based events (Houtenville & Conway, 2008). In addition, once children learn concepts in the native language, it is much easier to learn the new terms in English. Encourage families to explain to their children what they are doing and why during daily activities, such as housecleaning, cooking, gardening, or car repairs. Younger children can identify colors as family members are doing laundry. If a family member is fixing a leak in a pipe, the child can help hand the parent the needed tools and materials. Although the parent would be speaking in the native language, this example is given in English for ease of understanding. The parent might ask for the Teflon tape and then explain that it is placed in areas where two pipes come together to keep the water from leaking out. Or the parent might ask for a pipe wrench and explain how it is used to tighten the fittings that hold the pipes together, while pointing to the fittings. Family members should understand that explanations such as these, using as specific words as possible, improve the child's listening skills and expand background knowledge and vocabulary that later can be applied to English reading and writing.

Another way that families can support their children's education is by asking specific questions. For example, many adults ask children how their day was at school and the child answers "fine." Therefore, more specific questions are needed. Educators can help families by providing questions in their native language and providing information about their child's schedule that may assist in asking appropriate questions. For example, if the parent knows the child goes to the science lab on Thursdays, he can ask what the child did in the science lab that day. Other examples of questions would be: What did you write about today? What did the teacher read to you today? What did you do with other students in your class today? When the child answers, family members should be encouraged to ask follow-up questions so the child will expand the answer. Explain to families that this shows their children that they value what goes on in school. It also improves their children's communication skills in their native language.

All families also can share songs, poems, or stories in their native language. Help families understand that concepts and vocabulary developed in the native language can easily be transferred to English at school. If a young child brings an English picture book home from school, a family member and the child can make up a story in their native language to go with the pictures. This helps the child's vocabulary, concept knowledge, and understanding of story structure. For older children who are already reading longer text in English, family members can be provided with generic questions in their native language to ask the child about narrative or informational texts (Delgado-Gaitan, 2004). For example, they might ask about characters and the challenges they face in a story or about main ideas in an informational text or how both types of text relate to the child's own life or something she has read before.

Most families of ELLs recognize their limitations in assisting their children with schoolwork and will take advantage of help when it is available (Delgado-Gaitan, 2004). The authors and their college students had an after-school tutoring program at a local public school. Once the families found out about the program, there was a waiting list to get in. Families of English language learners made sure that their children came every week because the limited spots would be taken by someone else if they missed more than once. Although the program was designed to assist students with reading and writing, families often asked tutors to help their child with math or other homework; explain a letter or report that had come home from school; or discuss what a person needed to do to get into college. Thus, if schools provide assistance for families of ELLs, they will take advantage of the help. This assistance may come in the form of other parents, community volunteers, high school or college students who volunteer to help, or organizations such as the Boys and Girls Club. Information about the assistance program should be provided in the native languages of the community and efforts should be made to find bilingual parents who will pass the word on to other families who speak the same native language.

The best way to help families continue the momentum at home is to ask them about their needs and challenges. That is exactly how an innovative technology program began at Luther Burbank High School in Sacramento, California (Ferlazzo and Hammond, 2009). Large numbers of ELLs from Hmong background entered the high school when the last refugee camps in Thailand were closed in 2005. Teachers decided to use online audio books as part of their English learning program. During school events, the Hmong students had demonstrated the computer websites to their families. When teachers and translators made home visits, family members indicated that they would like to be able to work on the computers with their children but had no transportation to get to the computer lab at the school. Thus began the Family Literacy Project, guided by parent leaders. The high school was replacing its computers and had old computers that it could loan to families. A private foundation provided a grant for DSL Internet connections. Later funding was found for newer computers and wireless connections. Family members realized that the program depended on its success and came up with guidelines for families interested in having a computer and Internet access at home. Eighty percent of household members had to agree to use the computer for literacy purposes at least one hour per day and record usage on a log. If desired, all family members could use the computer at the same time in order to support each other's learning and discuss the text together. The computers were available for other uses during the rest of the day. Students whose families participated in the program showed four times greater improvement in English literacy than students who did not participate. In addition, younger and older members of the household learned English and provided support for each other, truly keeping the momentum going at home. The details of the program are not as important as the model it provides for family engagement. The program began with the requests of families and was guided by family leaders. (See websites.) This resulted in families actually using the computers for their intended purposes. Too often, educators set up well-meaning programs for families of ELLs but have low levels of participation.

When the process begins with the families and is implemented by families, higher levels of participation are much more likely.

In addition, the following activities help to make the connection between home and school without requiring extensive time or resources. More than one day should always be provided so that busy families have an opportunity to complete the assignments without adding additional stress to their lives. These ideas can be modified in many ways to fit into the curriculum. It also is important to understand the home cultures of students at your school so that assignments do not conflict with their beliefs. For example, some cultures do not believe in taking photographs of people, so a child may not take photographs of people even if the teacher is able to send a camera home with the child.

Activity
Clothes from Around the World

Purpose: Clothes found in stores in the United States are made in many parts of the world. A quick check identified clothes made in China, Honduras, Mexico, Pakistan, Vietnam, the United Arab Emirates, Macao, and the Northern Mariana Islands as well as mainland United States. Many families of English language learners also have clothing that they bought in their home country. Children can check their own homes with a family member to see if they can find a piece of clothing made in another part of the world. This involves family members with their child and the homework but doesn't require special resources or extensive time at home.

Participants: Student and a family member. This activity is appropriate for 2nd grade through high school.

Preparation and Resources: If possible, notes should go home explaining the homework in the home language. A large map of the world should be placed on a bulletin board. Bring a few extra pieces of clothing to school so children can practice looking for the location where the article of clothing was made before doing it at home. Yarn, push pins, and note cards are needed, as are access to the Internet, books, or other reference materials about different parts of the world.

Description of Activity: The student and a family member find a piece of clothing at home that came from another part of the world. (Students should have more than one night to complete the homework since the family may be too busy to complete the homework on one particular evening.) The student brings the piece of clothing to school and finds the location on the map. The location is then marked on the map, and a piece of yarn is extended to a notecard, where the child's name is written. The card should be big enough to include several names if needed. The student is then asked to do research on that country through the Internet or books that are available at school. Students should not be asked to do research outside of school because they may not have the resources at home or be able to get to the public library. The student shares what they find with the class and with their family.

Options: Depending on the age of the children, the teacher may want to write standard questions for the students to answer about the country or may want to allow them to write their own questions. Student presentations can be brief or extensive, depending on the time available and the abilities of the children. For example, students could make a travel brochure for the country or they could be a press secretary for the county and answer other students' questions during a press conference. High school students even could do a presentation targeted at companies interested in investing in the country.

Activity
Nutrition and Health

Purpose: Nutrition and health are important to students and their families. This activity helps students become more aware of nutritional facts of the foods they commonly eat at home and involves families in the student's investigation.

Participants: Students and a family member. This activity can be modified for prekindergarten through high school.

Preparation: If possible, notes should go home explaining the homework in the home language. The teacher may want to begin the unit on food and nutrition before students get items from home. The teacher needs a large chart with the food groups labeled and with space for students to write in at the students' level. Internet access, books, or other materials about nutrition should be available.

Description of Activity: A student and a family member find one nonperishable food item in a box, bag, or can for the student to bring to school. The student shares the item from home with the class. The class then determines where the item fits on the food chart and the student writes or draws it in the correct spot on the chart. The child takes the food item home and tells the family where he/she put it on the chart. Upper elementary, middle school, and high school students can share information from the nutritional label. Items also can be categorized by their fat, sodium, carbohydrate, fiber, sugar, protein, vitamin, and mineral content. After information is collected on a number of food items, the class can discuss how they could create a balanced meal with the items shared.

Options: After students have studied the nutritional content of food, ask them to find something that is high in a specific characteristic, such as sodium, sugar, or protein. Students can compare the nutritional characteristics of similar items, such as tuna packed in water with tuna packed in oil; crackers with cookies; or kidney beans with black beans. Students can also be encouraged to go to the grocery store with family members and help them find low-cost, nutritional foods. Teachers can give students a worksheet on which they copy down nutritional information at home rather than bringing the item to school.

Activity
Vocabulary Expansion from Home

Purpose: This activity encourages students to learn the names of everyday items they have in their homes and find out how they are used. Thus, it promotes conversation among family members. This activity is based on suggestions made in *Classrooms that Work* by Cunningham and Allington (2011).

Participants: Students and family members, prekindergarten through high school

Preparation and Resources: If possible, notes should be sent in the home language explaining the homework assignment. Teachers will need a camera, computer, printer with colored ink, index cards, and space on the wall or bulletin board to display the photos and captions.

Description of Activity: The teacher will ask the student to find a particular type of item at home. The student and a family member will then try to find one of these items at home and discuss how it is used. Examples for categories include: kitchen implements, tools, balls, batteries, soaps, things made of metal or wood, homemade items, and many more. The student will then share the item with the class and discuss how it is used in his or her home. For example, one child may say her mom uses a rolling pin for tortillas while another may say his dad uses it for pies. Thus, everyone's vocabulary and background knowledge expand. Students make personal connections to the vocabulary. A digital photograph is taken of the item and printed out. The child writes the name of the item and how it is used on an index card, which is placed under the photo on the bulletin board. Assign different children different days to bring in their items so that 20 or more children are not trying to share their item in one day.

Options: The teacher can identify an item in the classroom, such as "hinges" on the door, which may be a term the child does not know. The child can then share the English term with his family and ask what the term is in their home language if it is not known. They can then count how many they have in the house or apartment together. Young students may be asked to bring an item, picture, or drawing of something that begins with a specific sound, thus reinforcing the phonics lesson from class.

If you have a family member who would like to volunteer at school but doesn't speak English, he or she can help take photographs, print them out, and place them on the bulletin board. The family member can even put the name for the item in his or her home language on the index card along with the English name.

Activity
Family Interviews

Purpose: People have busy lives, and few take time to really talk with their children. This activity encourages children to speak with older members of the family, including parents, grandparents, or other people who are important to them.

Participants: Student and an older family member. This activity is appropriate for third grade through high school.

Preparation and Resources: Either the school or students should prepare questions in the home language in advance. Students will need paper and pencil.

Description of Activity: The student asks questions of an older family member. These questions may be about what school was like when they were a child, what type of work they have done, what they did with their friends when they were young, what things have been invented since they were a child, where they grew up, or anything else of interest. The student should only ask a few questions at a time, so this may be an activity that is repeated with different questions throughout the year. The student takes notes of the family member's responses in either the home language or English. The student next writes up what he or she learned in his or her home language or English and shares it with the teacher. If the interview is not written in English, the student translates the interview into English and shares it with the class. If there is someone else in the class who shares the same native language, those students may want to work together on translating their interviews.

Options: Students can take turns taking a recorder home so they can record their interviews.

They could also take turns taking a digital camera home to take photographs of the family member and something he or she does. These photographs can then be printed and placed with the interview. Students can do additional research on one aspect of the interview. For example, the student can learn about one of the inventions that occurred in that person's lifetime or about the community where that person was born.

Activity
Saving Money

Purpose: Most families will be really excited about participating in this activity which is designed to reduce energy usage at home. Some of the optional activities can involve students in other ways of saving money at home, too.

Participants: Teachers, family members, and students. This activity is designed for students in third grade through high school.

Preparation and Resources: This activity is best included in a unit about the environment or energy use. If possible, have a representative from an electric or gas company come to the school to discuss cutting down on energy usage. A letter about the project should be sent home in the student's native language. Materials should be available about average energy usage, no- or low-cost means of cutting energy usage, and more expensive options.

Description of Activity: The students should obtain a copy of an electric or gas bill. They then should compare their family's bill to average usage for similar families and similar home/apartments. Students should learn about free ways of reducing energy usage such as turning off the TV when no one is in the room or turning air conditioning to a higher temperature or heating to a lower temperature, especially when the family is not home or asleep. Students can keep a journal of steps taken at home to reduce energy usage. They can learn about low cost ways of reducing energy bills, such as putting weather stripping around doors, as well as more expensive options such as replacing older appliances with more energy efficient ones. Students can share these ideas with the family and decide whether the savings would be worth the cost for their family. Again, they can record the decisions in their energy journals. If time allows, students can compare an energy bill after these steps have been taken with one from before.

Options: Similar activities can be done with water usage, cell phone bills, gasoline costs, and other parts of the family budget.

Activity
Buddy Bag

Purpose: The buddy bag is a backpack that includes a book, a CD, a CD player, and materials for an activity related to the story. The books can be in English or the native language, or be bilingual. Some families of ELLs reported learning English alongside their child as they listened to the stories and followed along in the book. The idea was provided to us by Rosemary Roberts, a librarian at the First Baptist School in Brownsville, Texas.

Participants: Librarian, students, and family members. This activity is designed for students in prekindergarten through second grade.

Preparation and Resources: Gather backpacks, books with CDs, sturdy and inexpensive CD players, instructions and materials for book-related activities. Prepare buddy bags and explain them to families. Policies for check out and return of buddy bags should be established.

Description of Activity: Sessions are conducted at different times to explain the buddy bags to family members and the family's responsibilities in the family's home language. Students check out one buddy bag at a time. They listen to the CD and follow along in the book with a family member present if possible. The student then gets the family member to sign a paper that she listened to the CD and followed along in the book.

Options: Begin the activity with just one grade level, such as first grade, to limit the materials that need to be purchased. Many textbook publishers produce CDs to go with their science or social studies textbooks. Buddy bags can be made with the CDs, textbooks, and a family log to allow students who are having trouble reading the books an extra opportunity to listen to them at home. Involve family volunteers in coming up with ideas for the activities in the Buddy Bags.

Activity
Grocery Store Math

Purpose: The grocery store offers many opportunities to develop math concepts ranging from basic counting to more complex percentages. This should be done during the family's regular trip to the grocery store.

Participants: Family member and students. Activities can be adapted for prekindergarten through high school.

Preparation and Resources: Notes should be sent home in the native language explaining the assignment. The teacher may also want to provide a special sheet for recording findings. Students will need paper and pencil and perhaps a calculator.

Description of Activity: The student goes to the grocery store with the family member. Based on the instructions sent home, the family member asks the student to do math related to the shopping (see options below). The student reports back to the teacher what they did at the grocery store.

Options: There are many options for activities, such as:

- Young students can be asked to count items. For example, the family member may say they need five apples and the child finds and counts five apples.
- Have students weigh fruits and vegetables sold by the pound and determine what the cost will be for the amount being purchased.
- Older students can be taught to look at prices per ounce on signs and compare them for similar products.
- Students can determine how much is needed of items. For example, if two hot dog buns are needed for each member of a six-person family and the buns come in packages of eight, how many packages do you need to buy?
- Determine the price of items after taking the advertised discount. For example, if an item is 20 percent off, what will be the price of the item after taking off the 20 percent?
- Determine the price of items after taking a coupon discount. How does this price compare to other brands without the coupon?
- Use a calculator and keep track of the total cost of items placed in the cart. How does this compare to the actual cost at checkout?

Activity
Online Read-Alouds

Purpose: The idea for this activity came from the Family Literacy Project in Sacramento, California. (See websites.) It requires families to have access to computers and the Internet. This project is best to make voluntary for families who have access to computers and Internet at home or have transportation to computers at school, a library, or at a public location, such as a community center.

Participants: Family members and student

Preparation and Resources: Students and family members should be introduced to the website and how to use it. If the school is providing computers to families, guidelines for the distribution and use of the computers should be established with families.

Description of Activity: Go to www.storylineonline.net. This website has stories for children read by members of the Screen Actors Guild. The text and pictures are visible as the actors read the stories aloud. Choose a story and listen to it. Complete related activities if desired.

Options: Have families complete a log of stories and activities. Provide other free Internet sites where families can see the text as it is read aloud.

Activity
Community Involvement

Purpose: Community involvement projects can help create bridges among families, community organizations, and schools. They are best tied into topics being studied in courses at school but should not be used as part of a grade since some families may not be able to participate. Some projects such as planting at parks or natural areas or sorting food at the food bank may not require a great deal of English. Other projects such as distributing information or collecting information from neighbors or others who speak their home language may empower families and meet community needs. Some projects, such as a park cleanup, may take one day, while others, such as an energy project, may take a semester or a year to complete.

Participants: Middle school or high school students and their families, or younger students and families with appropriate modifications; community organizations and educators

Preparation: Someone at the school must contact community organizations and plan a joint project together that is appropriate for ELL students and their families. Students and their families can assist with planning this project as well as implementation.

Description of Activity: This activity involves information distribution and collection about winter heating costs and assistance programs. Other alternative projects are listed in the introduction and below under options. This could be done in conjunction with government, economics, environmental science, computer, or ELL courses.

- ◆ Contact public organizations and private companies that provide energy, energy audits, and assistance with insulation and energy costs.
- ◆ Decide on the information that will be collected from families such as the type of energy used for heating, the cost, whether they are renting or own their house/apartment, and what efforts they have made to reduce costs.
- ◆ Gather information that could be provided to families about reducing energy costs and assistance that might be available.
- ◆ Work with students and families to translate the main points into their home languages.
- ◆ Decide how information will be distributed and to whom. For example, it could be done door to door or at community centers, churches, or at cooperating businesses, such as grocery stores.
- ◆ Distribute information and collect data.
- ◆ Input data into the computer and analyze it.
- ◆ Write up a report and distribute it to community leaders, energy companies, and nonprofit organizations that provide assistance related to energy use.

Options:
- ◆ Conduct interviews and take photographs of local crafts or artwork and use them to create an exhibit for the school, library, or local museum.
- ◆ Provide guide services at museums or natural areas in the home language and publicize these services with others who speak the same language.
- ◆ Measure air pollution or water pollution at various sites in the community and provide this information to appropriate agencies.
- ◆ Ask nonprofit agencies in the community for other ideas about ways ELLs and their families could assist them in short-term or long-term projects.

Resources

Multicultural Books

In *Crossing*, by Andrew Fukuda (2010), Xing Xu, an only child, comes to the United States with his parents in the hold of a ship. He is one of only two Chinese students in his grade throughout elementary, middle, and high school. Xing's only friend is the other Chinese student, Naomi. Life is tough for Xing. His father dies in a hit-and-run accident right before his eyes. His mother has to take two jobs to support them and is rarely home. Unbeknownst to Xing, his father brought him to the United States and made his mother promise to stay because of his singing talent. He never uses it until a high school singing teacher fosters his talent, and he becomes the lead in a musical. Unfortunately, the rest of his life is in a downward spiral. Naomi is no longer his friend, and he is accused of being a serial killer. The author, of Japanese and Chinese descent himself, has worked with immigrant teens in New York City's Chinatown and as a criminal prosecutor. Based on his background, Fukuda creates a gritty story about an immigrant who never fits in.

In *The Namesake*, by Lahiri Jhumpa (2004), the parents in the story are from the West Bengal region of India, and the children are born in the United States. The story describes the clash between generations and cultures over more than 30 years. The narrative includes some of the misunderstandings that occur with the schools, especially the use of Gogol's home name at school instead of his "good" name. The schools are unaware of the education the children are receiving at home, including weekly lessons in reading and writing the parents' native Bengali language. While the children are assimilated to American culture, the parents, especially the mother, are much more tied to their native India, and most of their friends came from the same area that they did.

In *Voices from the Fields*, by S. Beth Atkin (1993), children of migrant farmworkers tell their own stories in text, photos, and poetry. Although their ages and stories differ, there are repeated themes, including the importance of family and their home culture and language. Although their families usually are not active in their education in traditional ways, they constantly emphasize that their children should stay in school, learn English, and get good grades so they do not have to do hard manual labor in the fields as adults like them.

Websites

English language learners

http://larryferlazzo.com/english.html

> Larry Ferlazzo, a teacher of English language learners, provides links to numerous other websites that include information that may support English language learners and their families. The linked websites have games, videos, read-alouds, songs, practice exercises, and information on science, social studies, careers, and many other topics. If families can get Internet access at home or a library, they can find the help they need with this site.

Family engagement blog

http://engagingparentsinschool.edublogs.org

> Larry Ferlazzo, an expert in family engagement, keeps this blog up-to-date. It is an excellent place to find links to recent articles and to other websites dealing with family engagement as well as Ferlazzo's critique of related news items.

National Education Association

http://neatoday.org

> The National Education Association is a professional organization of educators. This website is an excellent resource for up-to-date articles on a variety of education-related topics that are in the news. The National Education Association also has information about grant applications on its site.

National Parent Teacher Association (PTA)

http://www.pta.org/Index.asp

> This website includes information on how to begin and run Parent Teacher Association chapters, information about public policy and laws regarding education, ideas for improving family-school events and partnerships, and a place where teachers and parents can share questions and ideas for family engagement. The free onsite search engine makes it easy to look up specific topics such as homework.

Stories read aloud online

www.storylineonline.net

> Members of the Screen Actors Guild read picture books online while showing the text and illustrations of the story. Each story is accompanied by lessons and activities. If non-English-speaking families have access to a computer and the Internet, this site provides them with a way to support their children's English reading success. Family members may want to listen to the stories together in English and then discuss them in their native language.

Other Resources

Cunningham, P. M. & Allington, R. L. (2011). *Classrooms that work: They can all read and write.* (4th ed.). Boston: Pearson.

Delgado-Gaitan, C. (2004). *Involving Latino families in school.* Thousand Oaks, CA: Corwin.

Dudley-Marling, C. (2003). How school troubles come home: The impact of homework on families of struggling learners. *Current Issues in Education,* 6(4). Retrieved from http://cie.asu.edu/volume6/number4/

Ferlazzo, L. & Hammond, L. (2009). *Building parent engagement in schools.* Santa Barbara, CA: Linworth.

Houtenville, A. J. & Conway, K. S. (2008). Parental effort, school resources, and student achievement. *Journal of Human Resources,* 43(2), pp. 437–453. Retrieved from www.unh.edu/news/docs/Conway_May08.pdf

Kohn, A. (2007). Rethinking homework. *Principal.* Retrieved from www.alfiekohn.org/teaching/rethinkinghomework.htm

PISA in Focus (2011, November). *What can parents do to help their children succeed in school?* Retrieved from www.pisa.oecd.org/dataoecd/4/1/49012097.pdf

physorg.com (2005). *Too much homework can be counterproductive*. www.physorg .com

Smith. G. A. (2002). Place-based education: Learning to be where we are. *Phi Delta Kappan*, 83(8), pp. 584–594.

Vatterott, C. Hints to help reduce homework stress. Retrieved from www.pta.org/ 2563.htm

7

Challenging Situations

Markos was a handful. Rosemary knew it. As a mother, she knew he was very active and very compulsive. The children's birthday parties she attended with Markos almost always ended with him grabbing a piece out of the birthday cake or with the birthday child's new toy broken in pieces. He wasn't hurtful or malicious; he just was into everything. In fact, his joy was infectious. He waved at all the neighbors and called out to them when they walked by.

Rosemary's husband was about 20 years older than she was, with grandchildren from his first marriage. He either let Markos run wild without comment or punished him with a belt if something especially important was broken. At home with Rosemary, Markos was a doll; he was always making a funny face to make her laugh. He also was quick with an "I'm sorry" whenever he realized he had done something wrong, making it impossible not to forgive him right away.

Rosemary had a medical degree from Mexico where she had practiced for a few years before coming to the United States. In the United States, her degree was not considered sufficient so she had to find work as a nurse. She was especially invaluable as she could translate for the doctors and was able to make suggestions for treatments. Despite her training, she was not quite ready when the assistant principal at Markos's school called and said they needed to set up an appointment to discuss referring Markos for special education. The teachers at the school thought he might have ADHD and that he would need medication to stay focused at school.

Rosemary was devastated, and although she was highly educated and spoke English fairly fluently, she had difficulty assimilating all of the jargon used in her first meeting with the diagnostician. She signed the papers to allow testing, but she had some misgivings. She had the feeling though that if they just let him move around a bit more and did not expect him to sit so long that he would be able to fit in in the kindergarten class. But she kept her mouth shut, feeling that the experts should be the ones to decide.

Challenging Families

School teachers and administrators are often challenged by families whose first language is not English. Working with these families takes a lot of work from school personnel to help everyone be satisfied. However, in some cases, there are additional issues beyond language that come between families and schools. Having a warm and open environment can often diffuse these confrontations, but not always. In addition, schools have to consider families that have particular needs. This includes families with children with disabilities, families with residency issues, families in poverty, and families who have different concepts of health care, including mental illness. This is compounded when these families are not proficient in English. Finally, dealing with angry family members can also be a challenge for schools.

Families With Children Who Have Special Needs

The process of determining whether a child has special needs is difficult for both the school and the family. Having a child diagnosed with a disability can be devastating. It can also be confusing as it involves both an educational and legal process. This can be especially difficult for families who are not proficient in English.

The referral process for children who are English language learners requires that the designation of the disability not be based on linguistic or cultural differences. Despite this requirement, English language learners are disproportionately referred to special education. In order to reduce unnecessary referrals, schools should work with families to better understand the child and the family context. Family participation in the entire referral process is expected under the Individuals with Disabilities Education Act (IDEA). Generally, parents, teachers, and administrators find language differences as a large obstacle in the referral process.

Language differences also seem to lead to some under referrals, such as to gifted and talented programs. English language learners sometimes worry that their children might be misidentified. For example, a natural response for a young child being placed in an environment where no one speaks his or her language is to enter a silent period. This nonresponsiveness might be identified as a sign of a child with autism (Guiberson, 2009).

Standardized assessments may be one of the reasons for over representation of English language learners in special education. Standardized assessments can be problematic for many reasons, including that they are not culturally appropriate and that they are normed using English-speaking children. The use of standardized assessments in Spanish can also be inappropriate when they are normed with populations that do not match the culture and language of the child being tested (Fletcher & Navarrete, 2003).

Families and school district personnel often have difficulties communicating needs during the referral and placement process. Many parents feel timid when approaching school professionals; parents will agree with professionals out of respect. Handbooks and procedural manuals often mean very little to families inexperienced with schooling in the United States. Family members who are undocumented may not want to interact too closely with district personnel, which also complicates the referral and placement process (Hardin et al, 2009). Families may respect teachers as experts on the educational process, but what many families value more than anything is the caring relationship that the teacher demonstrates toward the child and the openness to communication with the family. Although family members do not necessarily see themselves as experts in the area of special education, they do express a desire to know what is going on and why (Hess, et al, 2006).

Children and families with special needs have a relationship with schools that is defined by law. All children served in schools that receive federal funds are entitled to a Free and Appropriate Public Education (FAPE). FAPE requires that all children with disabilities under both IDEA and Section 504 receive appropriate services. One part of this process that can cause difficulties is that families have the right to due process if they disagree with services or placements of their children. They also have the right to representation by legal counsel.

There are many resources available online that can help both families and school personnel better understand how to navigate the special education process. For example, the National Dissemination Center for Children with Disabilities has a number of resources including some for families and in Spanish. (See websites.) The Beach Center on Disability focuses on empowering families to better meet the needs of their family members with disabilities. (See websites.)

It is always important to learn more about families' needs, but it is especially vital for families of English language learners with special needs. One school reached out to Spanish-speaking parents who attended ARD (Admission, Review, Dismissal) meetings at the district's high school. At the end of each ARD meeting held, a survey was distributed in Spanish to parents asking them what information or topic they would like to learn more about related to special education and their child's needs. For three months, survey data were gathered at the end of the ARD meetings. At the end of the three months, the survey results revealed that parents wanted more information about transitions. Parents were concerned how their children would transition from high school to work or college. Based on the results, the high school gathered materials in Spanish and prepared a presentation for Spanish-speaking parents about the issue of transitions, which were of great interest and concern to families.

Although this activity was conducted in Spanish, it could easily be modified to fit the linguistic needs of other families. Additionally, it should be noted that the survey was administered orally in Spanish to those parents who were not comfortable answering the survey in writing. This practice showed sensitivity to the literacy levels of the families.

The survey and follow-up meeting communicated to parents that the school was interested in helping them learn more about special education and was available to answer questions and provide additional information as needed. It is also an example of how a needs assessment can be targeted to a portion of parents who may have a specific need for specialized information. This experience underscores that the school cannot make assumptions that families are familiar with special education issues and practices when no questions are raised. Parents may feel intimidated by the group of highly educated professionals to whom they trust their children and not want to ask questions in front of a large group.

Scenario
Documentation

Ms. Johnson, the school secretary, has admitted six new children during the third week of November at Brunswick Elementary. For Ms. Johnson, this is an especially large number of new enrollments. Normally, she might admit one or two students per month at the elementary campus. Surprised by the large number, she brings it to the attention of Mr. Baldwin, the school principal.

Mr. Baldwin does not seem surprised by the news. He mentions that in the last election, Sheriff James from Jefferson County won the election with the slogan, "Every traffic stop will require documentation." "I suspected that some of the families from Jefferson County would relocate over here," Principal Baldwin explained to Ms. Johnson. "Please try to set up a meeting with the new parents ASAP. I want them to know that they are welcome at our school and that to the best of our ability they will be safe here at Brunswick Elementary."

Residency Status

The majority of English language learners in schools are citizens or legal residents of the United States, but some are not. School districts do not collect data on students who are in the country illegally, but Texas, for example, estimates that 3 to 5 percent of its students are in the country illegally and about twice that number have at least one parent who does not have legal status. Most came into the country legally and then overstayed education, work, or visitor visas. These families may be especially complicated when some members of the family have legal residency and some do not.

The Supreme Court ruled in 1982 in the case of Plyler vs. Doe that children have a constitutional right to attend schools regardless of their residency status. Schools are required to educate students who live in their service area. Under interpretations of Plyler, school districts can ask only for proof that the child lives within district boundaries. They may not ask about a student's residency status. Although the district intake center may infer what the residency status is of students and their families, teachers rarely do.

Yet a family's residency status may impact their interactions with the school. Family members without legal status in the United States constantly worry about getting caught and being deported. For example, they cannot obtain driver's licenses and so want to minimize their driving as much as possible. Some schools also require family members to show a driver's license at the front office to get a pass to go to classrooms, but these family members will not have that identification. Families often will not allow their students to travel for competitions or tournaments outside the immediate region. They are concerned the child's identification might be checked or that they might be deported while the child is out of town, separating the family. We know of cases where star athletes and chess players have qualified for state or national competitions but have not been allowed to go to the competitions by their families for these reasons.

In high school, the student's residency status may impact their choice of classes and career goals. Students without legal documents may complete high school courses for dental hygienists, plumbing, or nursing assistant but will be unable to obtain certification from the state without a social security number. In addition, adult family members have difficulty obtaining and keeping steady work, and these families often live in extreme poverty, even lacking electricity or running water. They may move frequently in search of better jobs. People without social security numbers also are not eligible for welfare or many other public services.

Undocumented families have been targeted politically and legally in many states. This may lead families to move to another community that does not have the same restrictions. Changes in federal policy toward undocumented families also shift frequently due to political changes and uneven implementation in different parts of the country. This can have a profound impact on children who have undocumented family members. Although one or more family members may be legal citizens or residents, when one member of a family does not have legal status it can lead to major disruptions in schooling. The National Association of School Boards and the National Education Association released a joint report in 2009 providing legal advice for school districts concerning undocumented children. (See websites.)

Children in Poverty

Although figures are not available specifically for families of English language learners, the 2010 census indicates that 15.1 percent of the population in general lives in poverty while 19 percent of foreign-born residents and 23.2 percent of all Hispanics live in poverty. Children of immigrant parents are more likely to be living in poverty. In addition, the schools that have large percentages of English language learners are more likely to be Title I schools and are more likely to have more students who qualify for free and reduced lunch (Fry, 2008).

Poverty can impact children in many ways that negatively influences their educational outcomes. Children living in poverty are more likely to drop out of school and are more likely to have academic difficulties. Children living in poverty are also more likely to have emotional problems, lower self esteem and peer relational problems. Children living in poverty often have more health problems due to lack of access to health services (Moore et al, 2009).

Homelessness is one aspect of poverty. Although statistics are not available for homelessness among English language learners specifically, homelessness is high among families living in poverty. Approximately one million students a year experience homelessness in the United States (U.S. Department of Education). The National Association for the Education of Homeless Children and Youth define homelessness to include "children and youth who lack a fixed, regular, and adequate nighttime residence." (See websites.) They may be living in shelters, cars, campgrounds, motels, on the street, or temporarily doubling up on housing with relatives or friends. Homelessness has a significant impact on the students and their families. These families are often very mobile, seeking safe and affordable housing or escaping abuse. It is estimated that every time a child changes schools, three to six months of education is lost and children fall further and further behind.

Some of the students are not in school at all because they lack of immunization records or proof of residency in a district. Many educators do not know that the McKinney-Vento Act's Education of Homeless Children and Youth Program require schools to allow homeless students to remain at the same school even if they have moved out of the school's service area or district, allow them to enroll in school even without proper records, and provide a district liaison to work with homeless students and their families. If you have homeless children in your classroom or school, find out who the district's homeless liaison person is and what services can be provided to the students and their families. Even though there are enormous obstacles to working with these families, school is often the only stable place in the student's life. School also offers the opportunity for these students to gain the knowledge and skills needed to escape the cycle of poverty.

Families in poverty often have informal networks to find services and goods that they need. For example, they might know which churches have food banks. Middle-class teachers and administrators are often unaware of these services since they do not rely on them for their day-to-day survival. One way schools can improve the lives of families living in poverty is by identifying community resources. (See activity.)

Health Issues

Health issues are another delicate area when dealing with culturally and linguistically diverse families. Language differences and different views of illnesses can cause misunderstanding. The Center for Health and Health Care in the Schools posted a survey about cross-cultural issues on their website. (See websites.) Some of the issues that most impacted the work of the respondents were language differences and differing attitudes toward Western medicine, especially behavioral and mental health issues.

For people like ourselves, who have grown up and are accustomed to Western medicine, understanding different perspectives on health can be difficult. Many cultures attribute illness to spiritual causes rather than biological causes. *Mal de ojo*, or the evil eye, may be the source of an illness, and spiritual or religious cures may be sought out before going to a traditional doctor. School personnel may not understand the process and view the family as uncaring when the family may be doing exactly what is expected in their home communities.

Attributions of illness may also impact schools. Many families view cold weather as a harbinger of illness. Schools that continue recess or outside physical education may find that families will keep children at home, to keep them from going outside. They may view the school as inviting illness by taking children outside in cooler weather. Wearing shoes is also a common protection against illness in many communities. Asking children to take off their shoes or allowing them to walk around without shoes can challenge some families' beliefs about the spread of illness.

The Center for Health and Health Care in the Schools has many recommendations for helping schools understand community health issues. The center recommends that schools provide written materials in all appropriate languages and literacy levels. They also recommend using professional interpreters for important conversations (especially health-related conversations). In addition, they recommend developing a parent/community advisory committee to help school personnel better understand the decisions families make on health issues. Finally, they recommend that, when possible, schools hire staff members who reflect the community served.

Angry Families

Not all families have positive feelings about schools. Some adults have had negative experiences themselves in schools. It is human instinct to try to protect our children from what we view as mistreatment by other children or the school. Family members also can be angry when they feel that the school is not meeting their child's needs or that their child is unsafe at school. Families are most involved in school when they are very satisfied or very dissatisfied (Zellman and Waters, 1998, as cited in Cristenson, Godber, and Anderson, 2005).

Angry families often have reason for their anger, and when channeled properly, the energy that went into the anger can be used to improve schools. When the anger is simply ignored, it becomes difficult for both the families and the schools.

One source of anger for families can be attributed to a cultural mismatch between the school and the family. The United States system of democratic traditions and respect for the individual can be difficult for families who have a different understanding of authority. Many cultures revere elders, have patrilineal/matrilineal systems of authority, and expect individuals to submit to familial needs. When families see school systems undermining the trusted system of authority, they can become angry. Embarrassing an elder in front of children may cause the elder to punish the children and distrust school personnel. Research into how different cultures treat authority can be helpful in improving school family relations.

Family anger toward schools can have negative consequences for communities, especially when many families stand together in opposition to school policies. With the advent of parent trigger laws in more and more states, educators and administrators ignore angry families at their own peril. Although the details of the parent trigger laws vary from state to state, they give families the right to intervene in schools that are failing. More than half the families of children at McKinley Elementary School in Compton, California, signed a petition to turn the school into a charter school because their children were continuously failing state exams in math and reading. By working to listen to families' concerns, schools can avoid getting to this drastic point. (See websites.)

For example, Mrs. Chung, a Korean parent who had a son in third grade, came to the principal's office at the end of the year extremely angry because the third-grade teacher just told her that her son would be held back because he failed the state exam. Mr. Sandoval, the school's principal, put off a visit to a teacher's classroom so he could see her immediately. He also called in the library assistant, who spoke Korean, to help with translation if needed. As the meeting progressed, he learned that Eric Chung, the third grader, had received all As and Bs throughout the year. Mrs. Chung was angry that her child was being held back based on the results of one test. If she had known he was having trouble, she would have gotten him extra help after school or on weekends, but now it was too late. Mr. Sandoval let Mrs. Chung finish explaining the situation in Korean as the library assistant translated. Mr. Sandoval said he understood Mrs. Chung's frustration. He then explained to Mrs. Chung that students who fail the test but do well in summer school are allowed to move on to the next grade. He asked if she would be willing to allow Eric to go to summer school. She agreed that this was a good alternative. Mr. Sandoval then accompanied Mrs. Chung to the school secretary's desk and asked him to help Mrs. Chung complete the necessary forms for Eric to go to summer school.

After Mrs. Chung left, Mr. Sandoval made a note to himself to discuss this type of situation (without names) with the teachers at their next meeting. How could a child get all As and Bs during the year and fail the state exam? Was the classroom work not aligned well enough with the exam? Was this the difference between teachers providing scaffolding during classroom work and their inability to help students during the exam? Should the school report the results of benchmark exams to families even if the results were not used as part of grades? Mr. Sandoval really did understand Mrs. Chung's frustration and hoped that with the teachers' assistance, he could prevent similar situations in the future.

Mr. Sandoval abided by several of the following recommendations for dealing with angry family members:

- Deal with the problem as soon as possible. Forcing family members to make another trip to the school or wait a long time for a meeting often makes the problem worse. However, there are times when family members are abusive or violent and need to cool off before discussing the issues logically.

- Know in advance what languages other than English your staff members speak and use them as translators when there are unexpected meetings such as this one. Even if the family member is able to speak English fluently, it is a good idea to have someone else in the room in case there are future questions about the conversation.

- Listen carefully and calmly to what the family member is saying without becoming defensive. Often family members just want to know that their complaints are being heard. Try to envision yourself in the family member's position.

- Ensure that family members are treated as an equal and valued partner in their child's education. This can be done by thanking family members for coming to the school and stressing that both the school (teacher or administrator) and the family member have a shared interest in helping the child be successful. Starting the conference in this manner helps set a positive tone for the conference.

- Refrain from using educational jargon.

- Work with the family member on a resolution to the problem. Be willing to ask for his or her thoughts and advice. If the problem cannot be resolved immediately, tell the family member what steps you will take to resolve the problem and provide a reasonable date when you will get back to him or her. Find out the best way and time to communicate this information. Sometimes it may be over the phone or through e-mail, but other times, it may require a follow-up meeting.

♦ Do follow up with the family member in a reasonable amount of time. We have all experienced someone telling us that they will "check into something" and never hearing back. This is likely to lead to families becoming angrier and more frustrated. Following up as promised helps build trust between the family and the school.

♦ Work with other stakeholders to prevent similar problems in the future. Those that are closest to the problem usually have the best ideas for solutions. This may include groups of parents, teachers, counselors, bus drivers, or other interested community members.

No one relishes dealing with angry family members, but it is important to remain calm. In some cases, such as in the previous scenario, angry family members provide insights into problems that might not otherwise come to light and provide opportunities for improvement.

Schools can also help diffuse angry parents by ensuring that all the staff deals with parents in a professional and courteous manner. School personnel must recognize that family members may have made a concerted effort to come to the school to speak with school officials about their child's particular situation. Special transportation arrangements may have been made such as asking for a ride from a friend, borrowing a car or walking with small children to the school. At times, family members may have even taken off time from their jobs, often unpaid, to visit the school. When families take unpaid leave they may be foregoing much needed income for family essentials such as food or utilities in an effort to attend to their child's needs. In these situations, family members are intent on having access to someone at the school that can help resolve their situation. Usually this is the principal. Also, at times family members may have asked someone such as a neighbor or relative to come to the school with them to help translate or navigate the school system. Schools may mistakenly view this as an intentional tactic to intimidate the school.

Families of ELLs, who are unfamiliar with the school system in the United States, may not understand why they are unable to see a teacher or principal immediately when they come to the school with an urgent matter. School staff should remain courteous and reassure family members that their concerns will be addressed in a timely manner and that access to an administrator or other educational professional who can assist with their concerns will be granted. Far too often, school staff says the principal is not available and that an appointment needs to be scheduled. Some schools regularly engage in this practice as a "buffer" mechanism.

Schools wishing to build trust with all families, including those who are culturally and linguistically diverse, should view family visits in a more positive light. When upset family members are at the school, school staff should let the principal know the angry families are present and want to speak with the principal rather than practice their buffer tactic. If at all possible, the principal should make an effort to visit with these families and empathize with the special efforts they have made to come to the school. If the principal is unavailable then an assistant principal or counselor should visit with these families. We, the authors, would suggest that school administrators at least greet the family members and explain why they are unavailable to see them at the moment and let the families know who is available to speak with them and that they personally will follow up on the situation. Or ask if the families can wait a few moments while the principal rearranges his or her schedule. Such actions communicate to the families that the school is interested in them and their concerns. This promotes and builds trust.

Consider the following example—a real life situation that occurred in a middle school. A sixth-grade middle school student broke his arm at school. The school nurse notified his mother at her job that her son had been injured and needed medical attention. The mother left her job to go to the school. The son explained to his mother that the injury had occurred when an eighth-grade student whom he didn't know grabbed him. No administrator was available to speak with the concerned mother. Only the nurse was there. The family did not carry medical insurance on the child and would need to pay out of pocket for an emergency room visit and other costs.

The mother arrived at the school the next morning to talk with the principal about the incident and her son's safety. Additionally, she was concerned that her son could not write class notes with a broken arm. The mother had made special arrangements to drive her son to school (rather than having him take the bus) and to show up at work late in an effort to talk with school officials about the incident. The mother was told by a school clerks that she would need to schedule an appointment with the principal's secretary, who was not yet on campus and that no administrator could see her without an appointment. She was told to call the principal's secretary at a set time later in the day to set up her appointment. This set time did not fit with her schedule, and she was unable to call the school secretary. At the end of the day, the mother left her job early to again try and see the principal. Again, no one was available to speak with her, and no one in the office offered to have an administrator call her back. As a result of this treatment, the mother was very angry and frustrated with the school. She felt that the administrators did not want to speak with her and did not care about her son. She left the school knowing that a call to the superintendent's office was warranted and that the school needed to make special accommodations to help her son's note taking. In this example, the mother was well educated, spoke English, and was familiar with the school system, as she was a teacher in a neighboring district.

Imagine this situation occurring with a family who did not speak English, was supported by a job that paid an hourly wage, and was unfamiliar with the operating procedures of schools. The family would be very frustrated and angry. The family had an injured child, high medical bills, and a lower paycheck because of missed work. The family would also worry about the child's academic success because of his inability to write. Why couldn't an administrator have taken the time to speak with them and understand the situation's negative impact on their family? Trust with the school would be damaged.

Schools should examine how easily families can gain access to the principal or other administrators to discuss serious concerns. Making access to administration an arduous and drawn out process damages the level of trust between family members and school staff and adds tension to situations that might be otherwise resolved in a timely fashion. Additionally, schools must always be cognizant of the impact that such situations have on the family as a whole.

School staff such as security guards and office staff may be the first individuals angry family members encounter on the school grounds. Some families may be very upset. The initial contact with the school helps set the tone for the school visit. All staff should be reminded that all parents are to be treated courteously and professionally at all times and to direct difficult situations to the administration immediately. Every situation is an opportunity to build trust.

Language as a Resource

There are about five thousand different languages spoken in the world. In the United States, language resources have frequently played an important role in our history. For example, when the Pilgrims traveled to North America in 1620 to start the Plymouth Colony, they were met by Native Americans who already spoke English. One of these was Squanto, who acted as a translator for them.

The United States military also has a keen understanding about how important it is to have personnel who are proficient in many languages. They actively recruit speakers of languages other than English, and they will train personnel who demonstrate an aptitude for learning languages. Personnel with knowledge of languages other than English help in communications, translation, and even espionage. School districts should check their own staff and community agencies to see if there are people who can help with translation, especially for languages only spoken by a few families in the district. (See activity.)

Conclusions

This chapter has covered a number of issues that may complicate school and family communication and the educational process. Having an understanding of other cultures and challenging situations that may arise can help school personnel be prepared and have a plan to build relationships even under difficult circumstances.

Activity
Community Resources

Purpose: The purpose of this activity is to locate community resources for families in need.

Participants: People with knowledge of community resources, such as social workers, police and fire departments, school counselors and nurses

Preparation and Resources: Contact personnel and agencies that may be able to provide lists of resources.

Description of Activity: Make a list of needs of families living in poverty, such as food, housing, emergency shelter, transportation, and health care of all kinds, including dental care, mental health care, and immunizations. Match up those needs with organizations in the community that provide these services, including social service agencies, churches, medical clinics, shelters, and civic organizations. Make a list of each of these resources with telephone numbers and addresses. Distribute the list to anyone who interacts with families. Make sure the list is kept up to date as resources in the community change.

Activity
Language Resources

Purpose: The purpose of this activity is to identify people already working for the district who speak other languages. Language may be important for district intake, communicating with families, and the ARD process. Districts may not be able to hire full-time translators for just a few families but there may be hidden "translators" already working for the district.

Participants: Everyone who works for the district from the superintendent to the night security guard

Preparation: Prepare the survey listed below

Description of Activity: The survey should have a space to enter a language and then an evaluation score for how well the person has acquired the language. Some people have skills in three or more languages, so they should be given the opportunity to fill in a survey for each language in addition to English. Below is a rubric for evaluating language skills. As a simple rule, we find that people generally underestimate their language abilities, so you may want to add plus one to all self-report measures.

- ◆ Level 0 Knowledge: You know what the language is and know people from the community who may speak the language.
- ◆ Level 1 Basic: You have survival skills in a language, for example you could catch a bus or train and order food in a restaurant in that language.
- ◆ Level 2 Conversational: You can follow along in a conversation although you may have difficulty with putting sentences together and lack some vocabulary.
- ◆ Level 3 Proficiently Literate: You can hold a complex conversation. You can read and write in the language, you would be able to write a note to a parent, although it might have some spelling or grammatical errors.

Resources

Multicultural Books

The Spirit Catches You and You Fall Down, by Anne Fadiman (1998), is the true story of a Hmong family with a child with epilepsy. The story focuses on the difficulties the medical system has interacting with the family. The Hmong family viewed the seizures as a spiritual experience rather than as a disability. The medical system wanted the family to conform to the drug regimen, but the family did not see the value of the medications. This provides a good example of how people from other cultures may view things differently leading to confusion of the roles of families and schools. This book has become an important text used in training medical staff in many programs.

Just Like Us: The True Story of Four Mexican Girls Coming of Age in America, by Helen Thorpe (2009), is a nonfiction book about the high school and college lives of four young women of Mexican descent who have been close friends since attending a Denver middle school. All graduate from college but two have legal status in the

United States and two do not. In addition to describing the personal struggles of the girls, the author discusses their families and the impact of immigration and legal status on their lives. Thorpe, a journalist, places these individual stories in the complex political and legal context of immigration in the United States.

Websites

Angry Parents

www.educationworld.com/a_admin/admin/admin474.shtml

> This is an article written by school administrators who have had experience dealing with angry families. It provides tips on defusing situations before they become serious.

Beach Center for Disability

www.beachcenter.org

> A parent support group that works to empower families in advocating for their child who has a disability

Center for Health and Health Care in the Schools

www.healthinschools.org

> This site has information about cross cultural issues in health care in the school.

www.healthinschools.org/Publications-and-Resources/Polls-and-Surveys/Web-Based
-Surveys/Caring-Across-Cultures-Achieving-Cultural-Competence-in-Health
-Programs-at-School-Survey-Results.aspx is a report explaining the results of a survey of school health professionals concerning cross-cultural issues.

Children With Disabilities

www.projectappleseed.org/aaceptance.html

> Project Appleseed has a 10-minute video for parents on an *Introduction to Special Education*

Colorín Colorado

www.colorincolorado.org/article/c42

> A portion of the Colorín Colorado site is devoted to ELLs and learning disabilities.

www.colorincolorado.org/articulo/14440

> This portion of the site has several articles in Spanish that can be shared with parents.

Family Network on Disabilities

http://fndfl.org/projects/pirc/index.asp

> A portion of this website is called "Parent to Parent." It matches up parents who have just found out their child has a specific disability with another parent who has successfully dealt with a similar challenge.

Homeless Children

www.nationalhomeless.org National Coalition for the Homeless

www.naehcy.org National Association for the Education of Homeless Children and Youth.

> These websites have information about educating children from homeless families.

National Dissemination Center for Children with Disabilities

http://nichcy.org

> Contains resources for informing families about disabilities in both English and Spanish

National Education Association and National Association of School Boards Joint Report

www.nea.org/assets/docs/HE/09undocumentedchildren.pdf

> This website has the joint report Legal Issues for School Districts Related to the Education of Undocumented Children.

Parent Resource Centers

www.fcps.edu/cco/prc/about.html

> Parent resource centers helping families with special needs children

National Dissemination Center for Children with Disabilities

http://nichcy.org/families-community

> Portion of the NICHCY site devoted to families and communities. http://nichcy .org/espanol/discapacidades/especificas is the portion of the website on disabilities in Spanish: Información Sobre Discapacidades.

Residency Status

www.ncpie.org/WhatsHappening/EducationUndocumentedChildren.cfm

> This is a link to a publication that answers questions about legal issues surrounding undocumented students in schools.

United States Department of Education

www2.ed.gov/about/offices/list/ocr/docs/FAPE504.pdf

> A simple government pamphlet on "Free and Appropriate Education." It covers who is covered and what services they are entitled to.

Other Resources

Cristenson, S. L., Godber, Y., and Anderson, A. R. (2005). Critical issues facing families and educators. In Patrikakaou, E. N., Weissberg, R. P., Redding, S., & Walberg H. J. *School-family partnerships for children's success* (pp. 22–39). New York, NY: Teachers College Press.

Fletcher, T. & Navarrete, L. (2003). Learning disabilities of differences: A critical look at issues associated with the misidentification and placement of Hispanic students in special education programs. *Rural Special Education Quarterly, 22*(4), pp. 37–46.

Fry, R. (2008). The role of schools in the English language learner achievement gap. Washington DC: Pew Hispanic Center.

Guiberson, M. (2009). Hispanic representation in special education: Patterns and implications. *Preventing School Failure*, 53, pp. 167–176.

Hardin, B., Mereoiu, M., Hung, H., & Roach-Scott, M. (2009). Investigating parent and professional perspectives concerning special education services for preschool Latino children. *Early Childhood Education Journal, 37*(2), pp. 93–102.

Hess, R., Molina, A., & Kozleski, E. (2006). Until somebody hears me: Parent voice and advocacy in special education decision making. *British Journal of Special Education, 33*(3), pp. 148–157.

Hosp, J. L., & Reschly, D. J. (2003). Referral rates for intervention or assessment: A meta-analysis of racial differences. *Journal of Special Education,* 37, pp. 67–80.

Moore, K., Redd, Z., Burkhauser, M., Mbwana, K., & Collins, A. (2009). *Children in poverty: Trends, consequences, and policy options.* Washington DC: Child Trends.

Whitaker, T., & Fiore, D. (2001). Dealing with difficult parents and parents in difficult situations. Larchmont, NY: Eye On Education.

8

Resources for Family Engagement

Danny Miller had been an educator in Georgia for 20 years. In the last decade, he had seen a great influx of English language learners, especially from Mexico and Central America. Although the families of the English language learners seemed concerned about their children's education, they did not come to many traditional school activities, such as the open house, parent teacher association meetings, or even Friday night football games. The students often lagged behind their native English speaking peers in achievement test scores.

Miller, now a superintendent in a medium-sized district, had attended a professional conference where he heard a speaker talk about family engagement as a way to close the achievement gap. The speaker even had ideas about different ways to engage families of English language learners. He brought the speaker into his district to speak with his principals and other administrators about a plan for engaging more of the families in the district.

After the presentation, Miller and the speaker left the room and asked the administrators to fill in anonymous forms about the parts of the plan they liked and the challenges they might face in implementing the plan. Now Miller was reading the comments. Almost all the principals believed in the things that the speaker was saying but one after another wrote that they didn't have the resources to implement anything new. They wrote things like, "My teachers are busy trying to improve the test scores of the students and don't have time to deal with the families too." "I don't have a budget to light, cool, or heat the building for families at night or on weekends." "My teachers are already stressed out by the new reading curriculum. I really can't ask them to do anything more." Miller realized that he needed to address these very real concerns before trying to implement his plan.

Although most teachers and administrators believe in family engagement, they are like the administrators in Miller's district—they just don't believe they have the resources to do one more thing. This chapter attempts to address these very real concerns.

The challenge to cut school budgets and expand programs with no new money is a financial reality faced by many school districts across the nation. Schools may not be able to rehire specialized staff whose sole purpose is family outreach. Crowded classrooms and limited space in schools may narrow the possibility for a family center. Funding for specific items such as printing and translation costs related to family newsletters may be reduced or cut. Such conditions make it necessary for schools to become increasingly aware of possible resources to support family engagement. Likely funding sources may include federal funds, grants, monies from community partnerships, volunteers, and fundraising.

It is important that schools not use lack of funding as an excuse to limit engagement with families. While additional funds may make family outreach easier, having the will and desire to build a sincere partnership with all families including those families who are culturally and linguistically diverse is the most critical. No amount of money can compensate for schools that view such families and students as a deficit or liability to the school.

NCLB

One major source of funding for engaging families in schools is the federal monies associated with the No Child Left Behind Act (NCLB), Public Law 107-110. Teachers and administrators need to work with their central office to determine which federally funded programs under NCLB their district receives, how these funds are distributed across schools in the district, and which funds are available for use at their campus.

Wording and provisions within the NCLB law emphasize the state, district, and school's required roles in building the capacity of parents to become "equal partners" in their children's education. Schools are encouraged to visit the United States Department of Education's website to become familiar with the law's requirements and related documents such as their nonregulatory guidelines, which help interpret the state, district, and campus responsibilities to parents. The resource section at the end of this chapter provides resources that are helpful in learning more about the law. Highlights of the law as it pertains to engaging families of English language learners are included here.

The NCLB Act was signed into law on January 8, 2002. (Renewal of the act has been pending since 2007.) Section 1118 of the NCLB law is specific to parental involvement and includes a statutory definition for the term "parental involvement":

> The term "parental involvement" means the participation of parents in regular, two-way, meaningful communication involving student academic learning and other school activities, including ensuring that parents play an integral role in assisting their child's learning; that parents are encouraged to be actively involved in their child's education at school; that parents are full partners in their child's education and are included, as appropriate, in decision-making and on advisory committees to assist in the education of their child; and the carrying out of other activities. (See websites.)

Within NCLB are many programs that have targeted funding available for qualifying schools to assist them with specific challenges related to improving academic achievement of students. The Title 1 Program Part A within NCLB is the largest source of federal funds for many districts. The purpose of Title 1 monies is to "provide financial assistance to local educational agencies (LEAs) and schools with high numbers or high percentages of children from low-income families to help ensure that all children meet challenging state academic standards." (See websites.)

Statistics from the United States Department of Education for the 2009–2010 year indicate that 56,000 public schools across the country receive Title 1 funds to serve more than 21 million children. The highest percentage of students are served in elementary school (59 percent), followed by middle school (21 percent) and high school (3 percent). (See websites.)

NCLB provisions require that 1 percent of the districts' total Title 1 allocation be spent on parental involvement if the district receives over $500,000. As mentioned previously, teachers and administrators in districts receiving Title 1 monies should ask their central office about what part of the 1 percent set aside for parental involvement is available for use at the campus level. (It is possible that the district may choose to combine resources at the district level for a particular initiative or parent resource center.) In general, funds are to be used to help build families' capacity to improve their children's academic achievement. Such examples include offering family literacy programs or training parents on how to use the Internet to communicate with teachers and access children's homework. Funds can also be used to help families remove any barriers that prevent their involvement. For example, schools may use funds to provide transportation and child care as well as costs associated with home visits. (See websites.)

It is important to note that schools receiving Title 1 funds are required by NCLB to develop a written plan for parent engagement with input from parents and community members. Therefore, families must be an integral part of the planning process and decision making related to how funds are spent. An assessment of what school families want and need is a critical first step in developing a school's required plan. The school needs assessment should seek to incorporate all families' viewpoints, including those who are culturally and linguistically diverse.

NCLB also requires that districts and schools provide information to parents of Title I, Part A students in an "understandable and uniform format." This means that "to the extent practical," parents must be given school information in a language that they can understand. Such required notifications would include information related to parent programs, meetings, and other activities. In particular, schools using Title 1 Part A funds to provide instructional programs to increase students' English language proficiency (bilingual/ESL) must provide specific written notifications to parents whose children qualify for or are participating in the program.

The NCLB Act allows for parental involvement activities to be coordinated among other federally funded programs, such as the Even Start Family Literacy Program and 21st Century Learning Centers. Schools seeking to identify available funding sources for family engagement need to become aware of all the federal monies coming into their district as well as become knowledgeable of all the parental involvement activities occurring across the district. Armed with such knowledge, schools have additional resources to support their family outreach efforts.

Fundraising

Schools may select to raise funds for parental involvement themselves. Parents, teachers, and administrators dread fundraising efforts even though most schools need to have some fundraising activities. Perhaps the worst part of these efforts is that most of the money goes to an outside fundraising company. A sure sign of how bad it has gotten is that one school sold "fundraising insurance" that gave families a card and a waiver from all fundraising for a school year. Fundraising can actually help build school communities. At www.fundraising-ideas.org, they have almost two hundred do-it-yourself fundraising ideas varying from catapulting pumpkins to kissing pigs and from pet photographs to competitions between high school classes for the longest paper school spirit chain.

Schools may wish to consider offering a free school movie night. Families who do not speak English and or have little money will view the school movie night as a fun nonthreatening activity at the school. Schools raise money through the sale of snacks such as popcorn. Families enjoy an activity that entertains the whole family and parents are given an opportunity to interact with families and school staff in a positive manner. This activity builds school community, connections, and relationships while raising money. Far too often, families view fundraising as the school taking rather than giving back. This activity offers a different slant on fundraising.

Recruiting Volunteers

With tight budgets, educators often feel they can barely fulfill their basic educational responsibilities, let alone provide services to the community. However, volunteers can help stretch the budget. They also help the school establish itself as a welcoming place and the center of community activities. Many years ago, schools depended on stay-at-home moms to volunteer, but few moms stay at home now and those who do often are caring for babies or elderly relatives.

The good news is that with the aging population, many people are retiring with extensive skills and relatively good health. They no longer want to be tied down to a regular job, but they also don't want to stay at home all day. Depending on their skills, they can help in the library or nurse's office, offer evening classes in English for adults, or organize after-school or weekend arts, music, or other activities that use school facilities. They may also help with clerical work or the work of teaching assistants, allowing others to have more flexible schedules. Contact retirement villages and apartments for independent living and target community programs for senior citizens. One school that made such an effort ended up with former principals and teachers coming to the school once a week to read with children. When one or two people have positive experiences at the school, they will help to recruit more people they know.

High school students are a great source of volunteers. They come from the community and often can speak the native languages of the families. Although adults need to be available for emergencies, high school sports teams in off season can help organize after-school soccer, softball, volleyball, tag football, or other teams at the elementary or middle schools. They can instruct younger students and serve as referees or umpires even for adult games. Many high schools have pre-nursing programs, and students in these programs can help with taking blood pressure, doing eyesight and hearing screenings, and handing out information to families. Students in various bands or singing groups can perform at family engagement activities. High school students may have a variety of special skills from animal care to car mechanics that can be tapped for family involvement activities. In addition, they have the energy and the language skills that may reach the families of English language learners.

College or technical school students are also an excellent resource for volunteers that can expand family engagement efforts. At some colleges or universities, there are civic engagement, community outreach, or service learning offices that help match community organizations looking for help with professors and students looking for hands-on experiences in the community. If this type of office does not exist at the local college or university, public schools can contact college departments that offer classes in the subjects where help is needed. For example, college students studying a foreign language may be able to help with translation of school newsletters for families. Some universities, such as the University of Texas at Brownsville, even offer classes in translation. Students studying educational leadership or administration may welcome practical experience in assisting with family involvement nights or activities. College students also can offer a variety of workshops for families at your school, including tax preparation by accounting students, helping your child to read by education students, or art classes by art majors.

Nearby universities may also have multilingual students studying in the field of counseling or psychology, and social work needing internship experiences. Such students may make an excellent source of additional support for ELL students and their families. In many cases, counseling interns are required to provide direct comprehensive counseling services for which families may have been referred. Brockton High School in Brockton, Massachusetts, makes such use of multilingual college interns. They work to link families to comprehensive counseling services, community agencies, and adult education such as ESL classes.

Ford School in Lynn, Massachusetts, offers classes to its parents on becoming a teacher aide in the school's classrooms. Upon completion of the training, parents then have the opportunity to serve as unpaid aides. Such service allows the parents an additional opportunity to learn English and provides a pool of trained classroom volunteers.

Service Clubs

Although service organizations often already have their own special projects, they may be willing to help your school or organize one-day activities. Almost all religious groups have service organizations; there are adult service organizations, such as Lions or Elks; and there are organizations for young people, such as Boy Scouts and Girls Scouts. Learn about an organization before contacting it and see where its services might best fit with your needs.

For example, Rotary Clubs are an excellent source of assistance for schools needing additional support in reaching out to culturally and linguistically diverse families. Clubs often choose to adopt a specific school and support it with volunteers and resources. Such an example is Wooldridge Elementary School in the Austin Independent School District in Austin, Texas. The school has been the West Austin Rotary Club's community service project for more than 15 years. Rotary members are involved in reading to classes, assisting with family literacy and math nights, mentoring individual students, and providing financial support to the school's family outreach efforts. (See websites.)

Rotary International and the International Reading Association (IRA) have formed a collaborative partnership to promote literacy worldwide. Local Rotary Clubs often look for service projects related to literacy in their communities. A useful publication at the site is the *Literacy Project Guide.* This guide contains service project ideas for Rotary Clubs including book donations, adopting a school, teacher training, early childhood literacy, adult literacy, student mentoring, and community development projects. (See websites.)

Partnerships

Partnerships offer many advantages. The work and costs of family engagement can be spread across several organizations. Foundations and agencies are more likely to provide grants to programs that are run by partnerships rather than a single organization. In addition, all the participating organizations bring different strengths and perspectives to promote the success of the program. They also have different memberships that may be able to reach out to different parts of the community. For example, some families may regularly attend religious services but do not come to school events. When the clergy announces a partnership with their children's school, these families may be more likely to attend joint events.

In order to receive funds from the Investment Capital Fund, a partnership of the Texas Education Agency and Texas Industrial Areas Foundation, schools must partner with community organizations that have a history of working with diverse families in the community. In Austin, Texas, a partnership was formed among Austin Interfaith, which includes 26 different congregations, the teachers' association, the Electrical Workers Local, and 12 schools, primarily in low-income areas. Teachers, school administrators, families, and other community members worked together to tackle problems of low student performance. At one of the schools, a school-based health clinic was established based on needs identified by families. A study by the Annenberg Institute for School Reform at Brown University found that the partnership resulted in greater resources for the schools, higher standardized test scores, more family engagement in the schools, and greater teacher-family trust. (See websites.)

Adopt a School Partnerships are used throughout the country to link schools with businesses and the private sector. Tuscaloosa, Alabama, has had a successful Adopt a School program since 1985. (See websites.) The program currently involves 57 schools and about 90 businesses. Although the roles of the businesses vary, the Tuscaloosa Chamber of Commerce lists six major areas for partnership: classroom activities such as tutoring or career awareness, recognition for student achievements, sponsorship of speakers and cultural events, recognition for faculty and staff achievements, donating equipment or participating in activities that improve the school environment, and sponsoring community involvement activities such as recycling or collecting school supplies for low-income students.

Another example of a successful partnership is the Family Reading Partnership in Ithaca, New York. (See websites.) The partnership has three major objectives: Encourage all families to read to their children daily. Make sure that all families "are able to own and borrow quality children's literature books." And provide books and support to families who "may not have found success in reading." The family reading organization is able to achieve these goals through a broad spectrum of about 240 partners, including businesses, community organizations, foundations and funds, government organizations and politicians, health and human service programs, libraries, religious organizations, and about 50 schools and educational organizations. Books are collected by a variety of organizations and at a variety of events, including sports events, and are then given out by health care providers and the Department of Social Services. Schools receive books to give out when families come to register their children for kindergarten. Ten different library associations make sure that all families have access to books to borrow, and the Tompkins Consolidated Area Transit works with the partnership on transportation. The partnership also brings together different organizations that may assist each other with other needs, such as the Homefinding Unit or the Food Pantries in Tompkins County.

Corporate Partnerships

Corporations are another possible source of funding for family involvement. Several examples of corporations that award grants or make donations to schools are included in this chapter. The list is not complete but is intended to be a starting point for discussions at your school about what corporate funding sources are available and appropriate for your school.

- ◆ **Lowe's.** Lowe's offers a "Toolbox for Education Grant" specifically for parent teacher groups. (See websites.)
- ◆ **McTeacher Night at McDonald's.** McDonald's restaurants offer elementary, middle, and high schools an opportunity to raise money through its McTeacher Night Program. Local school faculty take over a McDonald's location from 4 to 8 p.m. and receive a portion of the sales for their school. Families are encouraged to eat at McDonald's during this time period and see the school faculty wait counters and make burgers and fries. McDonald's restaurants in the St. Louis Metro East Area have participated with area schools for more than eight years and have raised more than $500,000 for local schools. (See websites.)
- ◆ **Target.** Target Corporation sponsors numerous partnerships with schools. The partnerships include library makeovers, books for schools, and a "take charge of education program," which donates a percentage of Target credit card purchases to schools. Target also offers grants to schools for early childhood reading programs, field trips, and bringing arts and cultural experiences to schools. (See websites.)
- ◆ **Verizon.** Verizon Foundation accepts grant proposals on a continuous basis from January 1 to November 16 each year. Verizon is the third-largest contributor to K–12 schools in the United States. (See websites.)

Many districts have professional grant writers in their central office. District grant writers may subscribe to newsletters and publications that provide information on upcoming grant opportunities throughout the year. Schools should contact the grant writers to explore what upcoming grants may be appropriate for your family engagement program.

Campuses may be interested in researching grant opportunities. The Internet is a valuable source for obtaining information about grants. Some websites provide comprehensive information, including step-by-step instructions and links to sites that offer funding ideas. Florida Atlantic University's Nonprofit Resource Center is such a site. The site contains more than 25 links with descriptions of resources to assist all levels of grant writers including first time grant seekers. (See websites.)

Other Donations

Teachers who need materials for projects can go to the DonorsChoose website. The website allows teachers to post their projects and donors can choose which projects to support. (See websites.) It gives teachers tips on the types of projects most likely to receive funding. The DonorsChoose organization then delivers the materials directly to the school. After receiving the materials, the teachers and students write thank you notes and share photographs of the materials being used. Since the program started in 2000, more than 225,000 projects have been funded. Families could be involved in choosing projects and helping with the thank you notes and photos.

The ehow website offers advice for accepting donations from individuals or businesses. The website includes advice on giving donors receipts for tax purposes and keeping accurate records for the school. (See websites.)

Free Parent Materials in Multiple Languages

Many free materials for supporting family engagement can be found on the Internet, including materials in multiple languages. Several sources are identified here so that your school can explore and determine which ones are appropriate for the families in your school.

The Ontario Canada Ministry of Education operates a portion of their website for parents entitled abc123. The website offers a variety of tips and tools for parents of preschool and elementary students including a list of "Tips" publications for parents. Topics available for download include *Tips to Help Your Child With Reading; Tips to Help Your Child With Math, Tips to Help Your Child With Writing, Tips to Help Your Child Do Homework, Tips for Sharing Family Stories,* etc. The publications are available in 15 languages: Punjabi, Urdu, Hindi, Chinese Traditional, Spanish, Portuguese, Tamil, Farsi/Persian, Arabic, French, Chinese Simplified, Tagalog, Vietnamese, and Korean. (See websites.) And as mentioned in Chapter 5, Colorín Colorado's website has reading tips in 11 languages that can be downloaded. (See websites.) Other tip sheets available from Colorín Colorado's website include: *Parent Tips: Help Your Child Have a Good School Year, Talk With Your Child's Teacher, Parent Guide: Who's Who at Your School; and Tips for Parent Teacher Conferences.* The Colorín Colorado's homepage also provides an option to view the site in Spanish. If you press on the button for Spanish, it also allows the reader to choose from many other languages and the whole site is translated into that language.

The U.S. Department of Education offers a wide variety of materials for families to help support their children in school. (See websites.) Some of the information is available in Spanish such as the toolkit for Hispanic Families. Six articles are included in the toolkit spanning preschool to high school.

Taking time to search the Internet will yield a multitude of free materials that your school can use to reach out to all families. Schools that are concerned about limited funding for translation or purchase of materials will find many brochures, articles, pamphlets, and more to support their engagement efforts with all families.

Activity
Making Connections

Purpose: The purpose of this activity is to find potential new partners and sources of volunteers.

Participants: Anyone interested in the school.

Preparation and Resources: Decide who will be contacted and what means will be used, such as in-person, written surveys, e-mail, or other means. Have a flyer ready that interested people can take into the community.

Description of Activity: Ask school staff and others interested in the school and their families what community organizations they participate in. This could include religious organizations, Girl and Boy Scouts, service organizations, gardening or art societies, museums, college organizations, or others. Then ask the participant if they would take a flyer to a meeting or a leader in the organization. The flyer would ask members if they would like to partner with the school, for contact information, and possible partnership contributions. The school may want to suggest ways that groups could help. These may vary from volunteers to clean campus on weekends to people who collect school supplies for needy students to others who sponsor special events on campus. Have someone gather these flyers and contact organizations that are interested in forming partnerships and make arrangements for the partnership. Although this will initially take some time, it will repay the effort in the long run.

Options: Ask staff members and families what businesses they have contacts with. Send out a similar flyer but include options for Adopting a School or contributing for specific projects, materials, or equipment. For example, some businesses may be willing to donate older computers or printers that can be checked out by students and families.

Activity
School Cookbooks

Purpose: School cookbooks can build a sense of community at a school, provide a learning tool for students, and even serve as a fundraising opportunity. However, educators should be aware that some cultures pass their favorite recipes down from one generation to the next by involving children in the cooking process rather than using cookbooks. For example, immigrant families from Mexico may find it strange to write a recipe on paper.

Participants: Family involvement coordinator or another organizer

Preparation and Resources: Decide how recipes are to be collected and selected for the cookbook. Find out how much it will cost to print and bind the cookbooks so that the length of the book and price remains reasonable.

Description of Activity: Invite families to submit a recipe for the book in their native language and then include both the native language and English versions for English language learners. The school may want to provide a theme for the book, such as vegetable dishes children will eat or healthy snacks for children in order to keep the book to a reasonable length. Choose recipes to include in the book. Get the book printed with a cover that will last through cooking.

Options: The cookbook can be used as a fundraising tool and to promote goodwill in the community. Here are some ideas:

- Sell the cookbook for fundraising, especially during holiday times.
- Give the book away to special volunteers, such as the mayor when he comes to speak to the students.
- If the cost of the copying allows, include drawings or comments from the students about the foods in the book to involve more families.
- Print limited editions and print a new version every year so families will get excited about the upcoming cookbook.
- Ask local bookstores to sell the cookbook.

Activity
Free Materials Research

Purpose: Providing useful information to parents in a variety of languages about school topics is essential for helping families become engaged in schools. A wide variety of free materials are available online that can be added to a school's family resource center or distributed to families throughout the year. The purpose of this activity is to identify those free materials and resources that would be of great value to the culturally and linguistically diverse families in your school community.

Participants: A team of parents, staff, community members, and teachers can be assembled for this activity. One team member should be designated team leader. A hint when selecting parents is to ensure that you have a cross section of parents who represent your school community. Be aware that some parents may feel uncomfortable accessing materials through the Internet and should be teamed with a partner who is computer literate. Parents who speak a language other than English or have limited English skills may be teamed with school personnel or community members who speak their language. Note this activity may be completed by a school's site-based decision making committee or advisory committee if so desired.

Preparation and Resources: Prepare in advance a list of family involvement websites and resources contained in the book. Provide each team member the list and access to a computer and printer. Decide how team members will be paired as they work through the activity.

Description of Activity: This activity will be completed in parts. Plan to set aside about an hour for each portion of the activity.

- ◆ Part I: Team members research on the Internet using the sites provided for free materials that would be of use to all families, especially diverse families, in the school. Members download and print samples of the most useful materials during the time provided. This portion of the activity can be repeated if more time is desired.
- ◆ Part 2: Set aside a meeting time as a team to discuss which materials selected by the members would be of greatest use to families in the school community, especially those families who may not speak English and have little familiarity with American schools. It is essential to solicit additional input from diverse families not represented on the team about the usefulness of the materials selected. Community members and families who speak languages found in the school community can be used to obtain this needed information and bring it back to the team. (Soliciting additional feedback will necessitate an extra meeting for this part, but such feedback is essential.)
- ◆ Part 3: Plan how to make the information available to families in the school community. Questions to consider include: Will the school web page be updated with family resources? Will printed material be added to a display of information for school families available at the school and in the community through local businesses, churches, community centers, etc.? Will teachers

hand out the information to families? Will the library contain a computer dedicated for parent use to allow parents to visit the online sites and read the materials?

Options: Teachers at a faculty meeting held in a computer lab could complete this activity. Teachers and staff would become familiar with resources available to assist them in building stronger relationships with all families. School administration could also feature websites of interest for parents in the school's weekly faculty bulletin and solicit information on an ongoing basis throughout the year.

Resources

Multicultural Books

Home of the Brave, by Katherine Applegate (2007), is a fictional story told in verse that reflects the hardships that many families of ELLs have suffered and their lack of familiarity with life in the United States, including the school system. Kek was in Sudan, herding cattle with his family and his tribe, when war broke out and both his father and brother were killed. He and his mother escaped to a refugee camp but when the camp was attacked, they became separated. A refugee resettlement center brought Kek to Minnesota, where everything was new from snow to indoor plumbing to money. He lives with an aunt and cousin, who also lost their family but have been in Minnesota for a while. His aunt works cleaning a nursing home at night and sleeps during the day. Kek attends a fifth-grade English as a second language class. Although he considers going to school a great honor, he misses his life before the war. Fifteen months after he comes to the United States, his mother is found and joins him.

Round Is a Mooncake: A Book of Shapes, by Roseanne Thong and Grace Lin (2000), is a picture book for preschoolers that takes them through the exploration of objects that are round, square, and rectangular. The young narrator of the story is Chinese. She identifies objects familiar to all children such as "round is the moon" and other objects unique to Chinese culture, such as "round is a mooncake." The book ends with a glossary of the shapes found in the book and a definition of their link to Chinese culture. For example, mooncakes are defined as "round cakes with sweet fillings eaten during the Mid-Autumn Festival."

Websites

Adopt a School

www.tuscaloosachamber.com/aas

Adopt a School webpage for the Tuscaloosa Alabama Chamber of Commerce

Annenberg Institute for School Reform

http://annenberginstitute.org/pdf/Mott_Austin.pdf

Building Partnerships to Reinvent School Culture Austin Interfaith published by the Annenberg Institute for School Reform

Colorín Colorado

www.colorincolorado.org/guides/readingtips

Reading tips for parents in multiple languages from the Colorín Colorado website, a bilingual website for families and educators of ELLs. www.colorincolorado.org/families/partnerships is the Building Strong Parent Teacher Partnerships section of the Colorín Colorado website.

Community School Funding

www.communityschools.org/assets/1/AssetManager/Final_Finance_ExecSum.pdf

This pdf file is entitled *Financing community schools: Leveraging resources to support school success.* Schools interested in funding community schools and making the most of their resources will find this publication of use. It is published by the Coalition for Community Schools.

Department of Education Parent Resources

www2.ed.gov/parents/landing.jhtml

The U.S. Department of Education's webpage listing numerous parent resources on supporting school success

www2.ed.gov/parents/academic/involve/2006toolkit/index.html

Toolkit for Hispanic Families developed by the U.S. Department of Education and parent information and research centers across the United States

Donations

www.ehow.com/how_4937648_receive-donations-schools.html

Article on how to receive donations. This article is part of a website known as eHow family, www.ehow.com/ehow-family. eHow family contains a wide variety of articles on parenting and education.

Donors Choose

www.donorschoose.org

> This website allows teachers or schools to post projects for funding. The donors then choose a project they would like to fund and teachers, students, and families can help write thank you notes to the donor.

Family Center Funding

http://dpi.wi.gov/fscp/pdf/fcsprntc.pdf

> *Organizing a successful family center in your school guide.*
> Pages 8–10 of this guide, published by the Wisconsin Department of Public Instruction, cover ideas for funding your school's family center.

Family Reading Partnership

http://familyreading.org

> Homepage for the Family Reading Partnership of Ithaca, New York

Fundraising Ideas

www.fundraising-ideas.org

> The site serves as a comprehensive site for informative ideas, products, and specific suggestions for school club and organizational fundraisers.

Grant Writing

www.fau.edu/~rcnyhan/images/grants.html

> Florida Atlantic University's Nonprofit Resource Center Grant Writing page.

Lowe's Toolbox for Education

www.toolboxforeducation.com

> Lowe's Corporation's Toolbox for Education grant information

McTeacher's Night

www.mcdonaldsstl.com/com_mcteachers.asp

> McDonald's of St. Louis and the Metro East's website on McTeacher's Night

No Child Left Behind

www.publiceducation.org/nclb_actionbriefs.asp

> The Public Education Network has published a series of action briefs related to No Child Left Behind. Users of the site can locate various portions of the law to review such as Title 1, Title 3, etc.

www.publiceducation.org/pdf/nclb/parental_involvement.pdf

The Public Education Network has published a specific NCLB guide, "Parental Involvement: An Action Guide for Parents and Communities." This is an excellent pamphlet that clearly outlines the legal requirements for schools' involvement of families.

www2.ed.gov/policy/elsec/leg/esea02/index.html
> Link to full text of No Child Left Behind Public Law 97-110

Rotary Club and International Reading Association

www.rotary.org/Rldocuments/en_pdf/factsheet_ira_en.pdf
> Fact sheet about Rotary International's Cooperative Partnership with the International Reading Association

www.reading.org/General/AdvocacyandOutreach/SIGS/IRARI_SIG.aspx
> This portion of the International Reading Association's website is specifically devoted to the IRA/Rotary International Partnerships.

www.reading.org/Libraries/Awards/2011_RI-IRA_Literacy_Project_Guide.pdf
> Literacy Project Guide featuring Rotary International and International Reading Association's collaborative literacy projects

Summer School and After School Program Funding

www.summerlearning.org/?page=funding_resources
> Funding sources for after school and summer programs webpage published by the National Summer Learning Organization.

Target

http://sites.target.com/site/en/company/page.jsp?contentId=WCMP04-031763
> Target Corporation's community outreach page detailing grant opportunities for reading and education.

Tips for Families in Multiple Languages

www.edu.gov.on.ca/abc123/eng/tips
> Ontario Ministry of Education's webpage devoted to parent information. Publications for parents are available in multiple languages.

Title 1

www2.ed.gov/programs/titleiparta/parentinvguid.doc
> Parent Involvement Title I Part A Nonregulatory Guidance from the United States Department of Education (downloadable pdf) Additional information about Title 1 is available at www2.ed.gov/programs/titleiparta/index.html.

www.projectappleseed.org/titlei.html

Informative page for parents on Title I legislation and parent involvement found on the Project Appleseed Website

Title III

www2.ed.gov/policy/elsec/leg/esea02/pg39.html

United States Department of Education's website for Title III Language Instruction for Limited English Proficient and Immigrant Students Section 3001

Verizon

www.verizonfoundation.org/core/education.shtml

Verizon Foundation's Education and Literacy page with information about initiatives and grants available to schools

West Austin Rotary Club

www.westaustinrotary.org/services

This section of the West Austin Rotary Club features information about their community service.

CPSIA information can be obtained
at www.ICGtesting.com
Printed in the USA
BVHW011057220421
605629BV00008B/180